(주)제효에서 지은 집

건축가 상상 속의 건물을 구현하다 I www.jehyo.com

925빌딩 / JHW 이로재 건축사 사무소_정효원 / 사진_문정식

DICKSON® awning fabrics,
natural protection against UV rays

딕슨의 기술로 완성된 어닝용 원단은 자외선을 100% 차단합니다. 햇볕을 차단하여 열을 조절함으로써 자연적인 환기를 유도하여 쾌적한 상태를 지속적으로 유지하여 줍니다. 딕슨의 첨단 기술과 우수성, 독창성을 웹사이트에서 살펴보십시오. www.dickson-constant.com

The new Solar Protection range

ORCHESTRA | ORCHESTRA MAX | SYMPHONY | OPERA | SUNVISION® | SUNWORKER® | ALTO FR

pumps up the colour volume!

딕슨의 차세대 오케스트라 원단은 향상된 방수와 저항력으로 더욱 안정적인 성능을 선보입니다. 딕슨의 연구개발 팀이 독점적으로 개발한 선아크릴 솔루션으로 염색된 오케스트라는 직조 과정에서 유색안료를 배합해 빛이나 날씨 변화에도 고유의 색상이 유지됩니다.

숫자로 살펴본 딕슨 그룹

· **250,000** 매월 처리하는 원단 롤 수
· **110** 전세계 배급 국가
· **11,000** 물류 공간 면적 (m²)
· **27,500** 생산 시설 면적 (m²)
· **110** 제직기 수
· **25,000,000** 연간 생산량 (m²)
· **75** 수출 비율 (%)
· **14** 전세계 계열사 수
· **100,000** 하루 총 제작량 (m²)

본방 B·O·N·B·A·H·N·G

서울시 강서구 공항대로 2길 18
Tel. +82 (0)2 2661 4321
Fax. +82 (0)2 2661 4323

DICKSON®
www.dickson-constant.com
Tel. +33 (0)3 20 45 59 59
Fax. +33 (0)3 20 45 59 00

World's Best
Architectural Ceramic

서초 미동전자 사옥 리모델링 / 운생동 건축사무소

배접보강을 통해 강도를 높인 무기질 박판 세라믹은 비산을 방지합니다.
평활도, 경량성, 내마모성, 불연성, 내염성, 내구성이 뛰어나 인테리어 및 각종 가구 마감재로도 매우 좋습니다.

THESIZE
NEOLITH

1200mm X 3600mm X 3mm, 6mm, 12mm

서초 경농 사옥 / 연미건축

Your New Playground

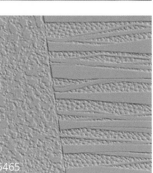

Norament 926 Crossline

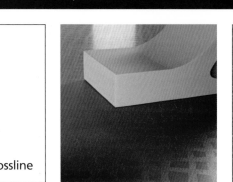

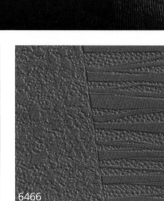

6466

6465

상상이 **디자인** 되다

세계적 디자이너 Lars Contzen의 작품, norament 926 crossline.
심미적인 디자인과 색상으로 당신만의 공간을 디자인해 드립니다.

nora®

세계 최고의 친환경 고무바닥재

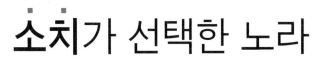

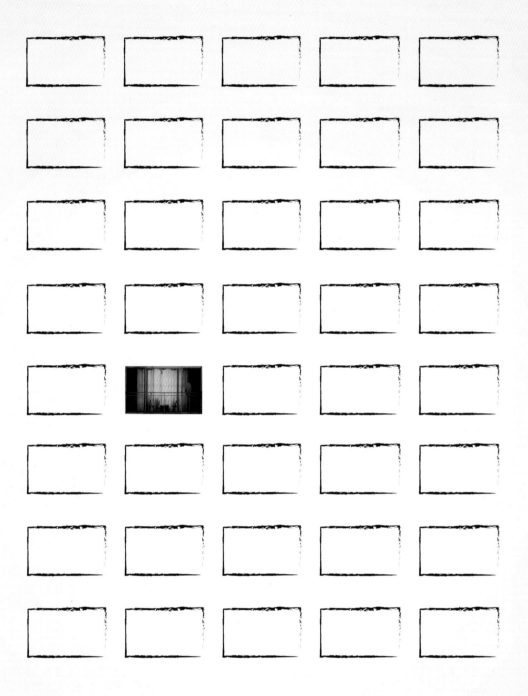

여백의 美

에너지사용, 적을 때에 더 아름답습니다

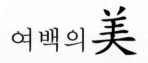

kobaco
공익광고협의회

품격있는 공간에 아름다운 소리를 더하다

공간은 예술로, 소리는 명품으로! 유공흡음석고보드 아트사운드

이제 아트사운드가 편안하고 아늑한 환경을 만드는 진정한 흡음 솔루션을 제시합니다.

아트사운드(ARTSOUND)는 예술, 명품 등을 의미하는 아트(ART)와 소리, 음을 의미하는 사운드(SOUND)의 합성어로 흡음 성능이 우수하고, 시공 후 공간의 미적인 효과를 극대화할 수 있는 유공 흡음석고보드입니다. 뛰어난 흡음 성능으로 실내 음환경을 획기적으로 개선 시킬 뿐만 아니라 공간의 품격을 향상시킬 수 있어 교육, 문화, 종교, 업무 시설 등 다양한 공간에 활용되고 있습니다.

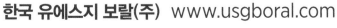

한국 유에스지 보랄(주) www.usgboral.com

서울시 강남구 테헤란로 87길 36(삼성동) 도심공항타워빌딩 7층
TEL: (02)6902-3100, FAX: (02)6902-3190

C3 No.385

Publisher JaeHong Lee   이재홍 발행인 겸 편집인
Editorial Director Uje Lee   이우재 편집장

Managing Editor YuMi Hyun   현유미 편집부 차장
Editor HyoJin Jeon   전효진 편집부
Editor JiMin Lee   이지민 편집부
Editor HyunA Jo   조현아 편집부
Art Director YilGui Yoo   유일귀 디자인부 실장

Contributing Editor Silvio Carta   실비오 까르따 객원 편집

Advertising Director ChangSoo Lee   이창수 광고부 이사
Advertising Manager SeungJoo Kim   김승주 광고부 차장
Advertising Sales SongBon Lee   이송본 광고부

Reader Service Manager YeSun Ji   지예선 관리부 대리
Accountant SuHyun Lee   이수현 관리부 주임
Marketing Director DoJin Choi   최도진 마케팅 부장

Printed in Korea   아트프린팅

ISSN 2092-5190   발행처 C3
Copyright 2016 C3   07622 서울시 강서구 공항대로2길 18 C3

C3 Publishing Co.   Editorial editor@c3p.kr
18 GongHang DaeRo 2Gil GangSeo   Subscription subs@c3p.kr
Seoul 07622 Korea   Advertisement ads@c3p.kr
Tel. +82.2.2661.2811   Distribution biz@c3p.kr
Fax. +82.2.2661.2456   http://www.c3p.kr

All rights reserved.   월간 C3는 한국정기간행물 윤리위원회의 도서잡지윤리강령 및 실천요강을 준수합니다.
No part of this publication may be reproduced   본지에 게재된 기사나 사진의 무단복사 및 전재를 금합니다.
or transmitted in any form or by any means,   1984년 5월 16일 등록 강서 라 - 00019호
without the prior permission of C3 Publishing Company.   1987년 2월 24일 제3종 우편물 (나)급 인가 - 우무 제532호

Cover Bosco Studio & House   ©Edmund Sumner

Guided Awning System

(주)정문건장
JEONG MOON ARCHITERIOR CO.,LTD
www.escudo.co.kr   경기도 남양주시 호평동 615-10 엠마오빌딩 2~4층 **Tel** 031 568 9013 **Fax** 031 568 9017

C3 no. 385

MODERN VERNACULAR
Bridging Tradition and Innovation

ARCHITECTURE IN INDIA
New Indian Identities and Architectural Tectonics

타일 이후의 타일

Post-Tile

**2016
08.09
12.25**
—

클레이아크김해미술관
돔하우스

클레이아크김해
ANNIVERSARY
The 10th

김혜경 Kim Hyegyung

김희영 Kim Heeyoung

네이튼 클레이븐 Nathan Craven

모하메드 도미리 Mohammad Domiri

몰리 해치 Molly Hatch

박성욱 Park Sungwook

수잔 베이너 Susan Beiner

이경민 Lee Kyungmin

이은주 Lee Eunjoo

주최,주관 CLAYARCH GIMHAE MUSEUM 후원
(재)김해문화재단 클레이아크김해

주한미국대사관 주한이란이슬람공화국대사관

CLAYARCH GIMHAE MUSEUM 클레이아크 김해 미술관 50874 경상남도 김해시 진례면 진례로 275-51 Tel. 055-340-7000 Fax. 055-340-7077 www.clayarch.org info@clayarch.org
Clayarch Gimhae Museum 275-51 Jillye-ro, Jillye-myeon, Gimhae-si, Gyeongsangnam-do 50874 Korea Tel. +82-55-340-7000 Fax. +82-55-340-7077 www.clayarch.org info@clayarch.org

C3 no. 385

Oernsro Timber Town _ C.F. Moeller Architects

With the "Oernsro Timber Town" proposal, C.F. Moeller Architects and C.F. Moeller Landscape, in cooperation with Slaettoe Foervaltning, have won the task of designing a visionary residential quarter in central Oerebro, Sweden. The competition was held by Oerebro Municipality together with the Swedish Association of Architects with the aim of creating an extraordinary urban quarter, as a "New impulse in the city".

Oernsro Traestad will be a destination and a vibrant quarter of Oerebro, with a clear idea of how to enrich the city's social networks by integrating nature into the urban landscape. The residential buildings interact with an urban city park including a variety of activities and plazas for social meetings and recreation. The buildings in the district will be created with solid timber frame structures, and will contribute positively to the overall lifecycle perspective of the project. Timber is a renewable material, with low energy consumption and a limited carbon footprint.

The new urban quarter comprises several apartment buildings of varying heights.

The activity route, or thoroughfare, through the area interconnects the existing promenade sections along Svartan creek with the surrounding quarter. Aengen, a generous public city park, gives the area an unexpected meeting between city and wild nature.

"We wish to create an including urban quarter in which the city's urban and social qualities interact with the park's organic structures. The proposal illustrates a vision with the objective to create an exciting place in Oerebro, of unique value, with innovative architecture," says Ola Jonsson, the project architect at C.F. Moeller.

"For us, it is an obvious choice to choose solid wood for structure as well as façades of wood. In addition to contributing positively to the environment, wood gives us new opportunities to create innovative and value-creating architecture. "

neighborhood/quarter layout

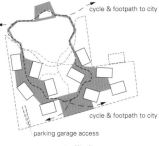

traffic flows

compact parking garage

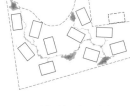

sustainable urban drainage

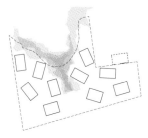

main public green

private gardens and entrances

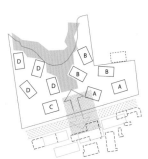

central access to the plaza
in relation to the future development

central axis and view to
urban/green from each housing

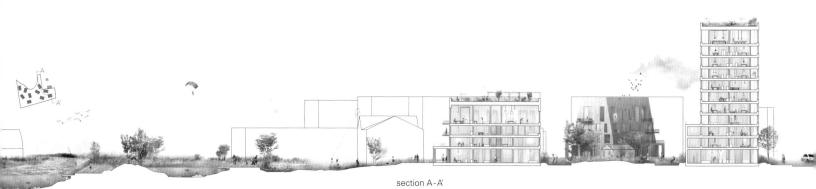

section A-A'

스웨덴 온슈 목조 마을

스웨덴 남부 외레브로는 한적한 전원 풍경이 인상적인 곳이다. 스바르톤 강이 도시를 가로질러 흐르고, 강을 따라 크고 작은 주택들이 줄지어 있다. 도시는 고즈넉한 분위기를 자아내지만, 오랜 시간 멈춰 빛바랜 모습으로 점차 활력을 잃어가고 있다. 그중 중심지인 온슈 마을에 도시 분위기를 전환할 새로운 주거 단지를 짓고자, 외베브로 시에서 공모를 열었다. 당선의 영예는 덴마크 건축가 C.F. 뮐러 아키텍츠에 돌아갔다.

공모의 목적은 도시에 생기를 불어넣고 보기에도 아름다운 주거 지역을 가꾸는 데에 있다. 건축가는 새로 들어설 단지가 주변의 자연환경에도 통합되고 도시 안에서 활력있는 장소로 거듭나기를 바랐다. 도시 안에서 거주민들의 삶이 자연과 하나 되며, 사회적인 교류도 왕성하게 하는 등 생활 전반에 걸쳐 긍정적인 영향을 주고자 했다.

따라서 강물을 대지 안으로 끌어들여 인공 호수를 조성하고, 그 주변으로 아파트를 유기적으로 배치했다. 건물들은 모두 목조로 계획했는데, 이는 나무가 탄소 배출량을 최소화하고 에너지 소비가 적어 다시 사용할 수도 있고 친환경적이기 때문이다. 새로운 목조 마을은 환경오염이 적을 뿐만 아니라 재료에 대한 높은 이해력으로, 도시 안에서 혁신적이고 새로운 가치를 실현한다.

높고 낮은 목조 아파트들 사이에 조성된 광장과 공원은, 주민들의 다양한 야외 활동을 돕는다. 또한, 강을 따라 이어지는 산책로와 인근의 양연 공원, 둘 사이를 연결하며 일상 속에서 예기치 못한 자연의 아름다움을 선사한다. 목조 마을은 색다른 주거 공간을 선보이며 도시 일부로서 자연과의 접점이 된다.

The Eyes of Runavik_White Arkitekter AB

White Arkitekter's 'The Eyes of Runavik' has won the Nordic Built Cities competition in the category Vertical Challenge. The Nordic Built Cities Challenge is an open, needs-driven competition for the development and visualisation of in-novative solutions for liveable, smart, and sustainable cities. In its 'Vertical Challenge' on the Faroe Islands, architects and engineers were enlisted to design a new residential area with infrastructure, landscape, and housing on a steep, currently undeveloped and uninhabited hillside.

Making Use of the Existing Site

The proposal is a literal composition of its local context, landscape and resources. Basalt rock, natural streams, strong winds, geothermal heat, sparse vegetation, and sheep wool are all integral building components that work within the wild landscape and vernacular architectural concepts.

Traditional buildings on the Faroe Islands sit on stone foundations, to counteract the steep slope_while allowing the heavy rain water to flow from the mountains past the structures. The Eyes of Runavik employs new construction techniques that in-

corporate minimal foundations that serve a similar purpose to the traditional foundations, allowing nature to envelope the houses, but are much less invasive. With almost no blasting or excavation, the natural contours are preserved and the native biodiversity is promoted. The circular settlements warp to fit the wild Faroese landscape, transforming into eye shapes as they individually respond both to the unique terrain and the prevailing wind. Even the contours of the green roofs directly reflect the shape of the terrain below.

Shelter from the Wind - Social Microclimates and Urban Farming

The wind is an omnipresent natural force bombarding the Faroe Islands from the open ocean, the narrow fjords, and the steep mountainsides. For that reason, wind analysis has been integral through the design process, resulting in the optimiza-tion of both the protective eye-shape and the configuration of settlements which best modulates the often violent wind conditions.

Where the traditional Faroese life outside of work goes on

inside the houses, sheltered from wind and rough weather, White's proposal aims to promote both stay in the outdoors and social gatherings in nature.

Living between Settlement and Outfield

The Eyes of Runavik establishes a set of principles and goals that are adaptable to a variety of steep terrains, but are specifically optimized for the social, climatic, and geological context of the Faroe Islands. The steep slope results in panoramic views to the surrounding fjords and islands, but also draws inspiration from traditional Faroese agriculture. The project explores historical modes of farming and settlement, where the outfield, 'hagi', is used for summer grazing, and the cultivated land, 'bøur', is generally used for growing crops. By adapting these concepts, the new development helps create a new harmony between the wild nature and the man made interventions in the environment. Each building ring - or 'eye' - can be seen as a settlement in itself, where the outfield 'hagi' envelops each building with raw Faroese nature, while the infield 'bøur' protects a cultivated microclimate in the centre that offers more inhabitable outdoor social spaces for residents to plant and interract.

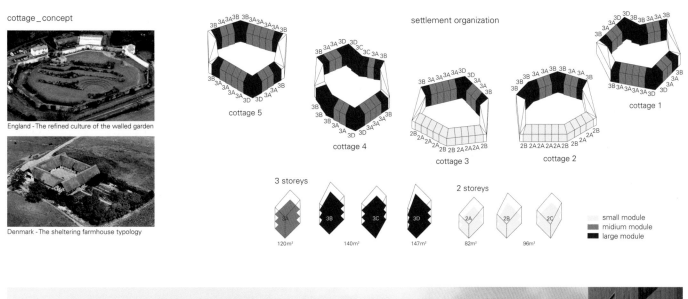

cottage_concept

England - The refined culture of the walled garden

Denmark - The sheltering farmhouse typology

settlement organization

cottage 5

cottage 4

cottage 3

cottage 2

cottage 1

3 storeys

3A

3B

3C

3D

120m²   140m²   147m²

2 storeys

2A   2B   2C

82m²   96m²

small module
midium module
large module

루나비크 비탈 위 공동주택

북유럽 지역 내 도시를 대상으로 북유럽의 기후와 지형에 적합한 도시를 제안하는 대규모 설계 공모전이 열렸다. 와이트 아키텍터의 설계안이 공모전의 '버티컬 챌린치' 부문 당선작으로 선정됐다. 이 공동주택은 덴마크 페로 제도 내 루나비크 지역의 가파른 언덕 비탈에, 주변의 자연 풍경을 아우르며 지속 가능한 주거 공간을 제시한다.

당선작은 부지의 지역적 특성을 있는 그대로 활용했다. 수려한 자연풍경과 함께, 인근에서 쉽게 구할 수 있는 재료들은 계획의 핵심이 되었다. 화산 지형의 풍부한 지열자원과 현무암뿐만 아니라, 언덕 곳곳에 흐르는 자연하천과 듬성한 초목 사이로 기르는 양떼의 털마저도 모두 주요한 구성 요소이다.

한편, 오래 전부터 페로 제도에서는 가파른 경사에 대응하기 위해 기초를 돌로 만들었다. 덕분에 아무리 많은 비가 내려도 건물은 피해를 최소화 할 수 있었다. 이 공동주택 단지도 지역의 전통을 활용한다. 그러나 새로운 기술과 공법으로, 최소한의 기초로만 설치할 뿐, 주변의 자연에 그대로 둘러싸이도록 한다. 발파나 굴착 작업을 거의 하지 않아 자연 지형을 보존하며, 토착 생물종의 다양성도 유지될 수 있다. 주거단지의 원형 건물 형태도 야생 그대로의 풍경에 맞게 재구성했다.

단지를 이루는 건물 각각은 독특한 지형과 풍계 조건에 따라 눈을 닮은 모양으로 고안했다. 바람은 섬에서 언제나 불어닥치는 자연의 힘이다. 사방에 열린 바다와 함께, 좁은 협곡과 가파른 산비탈이 일으키는 거센 바람이 공간 계획에 중요하게 반영되었다. 여기에 심지어, 옥상의 정원에도 지형은 직접적으로 반영된다. 이렇게 안에서는 삶의 전통이 거친 바람과 날씨로부터 보호받아 계속 이어진다.

이 주택 단지는 가파른 지형에 다양한 방식으로 적응한다. 그러나 무엇보다도 페로 제도의 지질적 특성과 기후, 그리고 사회 문화를 가장 고려한다. 급격한 언덕 비탈은 주변의 협만과 작은 섬들의 풍경을 전경으로 전망하지만, 동시에 독특한 농경문화를 만들어내기도 하였다. 전통적으로 루나비크 지역에서는 거주지 밖에 여름철 방목을 위한 목초지를 두었고, 안에는 경작을 위한 밭을 만들어 용도를 구분하였다. 이를 참조하여 자연과 인간 사이에 새로운 조화를 찾고자 했다. 주거단지 밖에서도 자연과 함께 지낼 수 있는 공간을 마련했으며 단지 한 가운데에는 공동체를 위한 별도의 텃밭과 정원을 만들어 거주자들이 모여 식물들을 기르며 다양한 야외활동을 함께 할 수 있도록 했다. 이렇게 만들어진 눈 모양의 각 건물은 자연 그대로의 들판으로 둘러싸인 하나의 정주지가 된다.

social function & activities

public/private

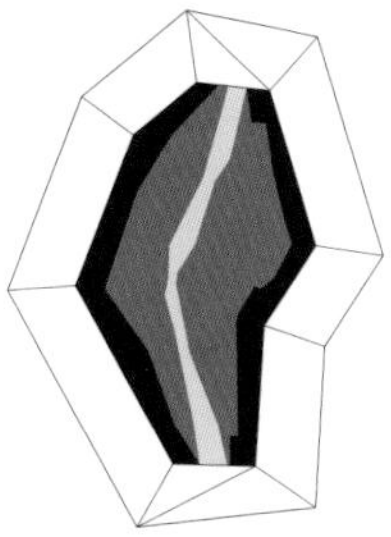

- public
- semi-public
- private

flow/accessibility

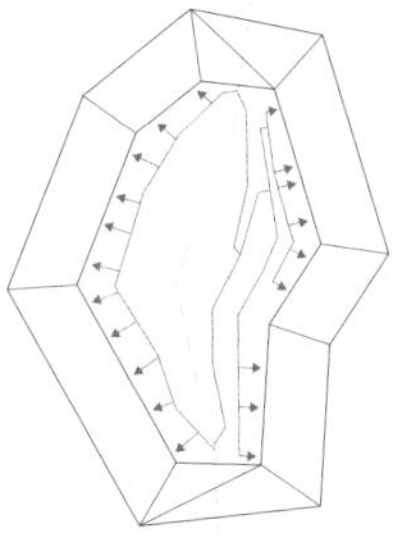

- main public route
- access to dwellings

activities

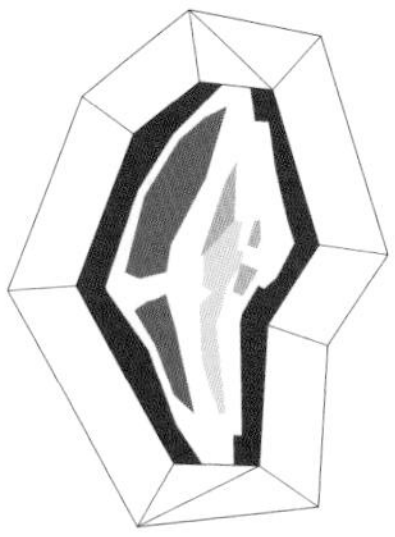

- terrace
- playground
- urban farming
- private gardens

community spaces

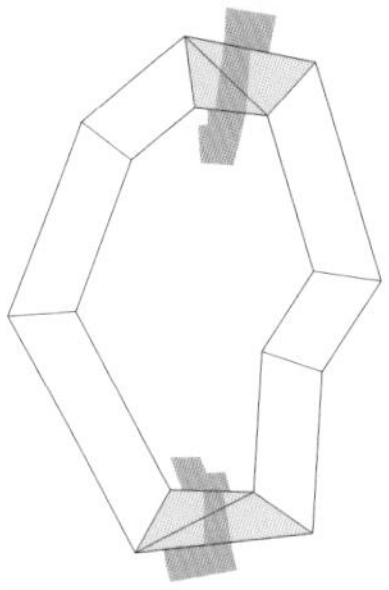

- community spaces
- communal terrace

plant species

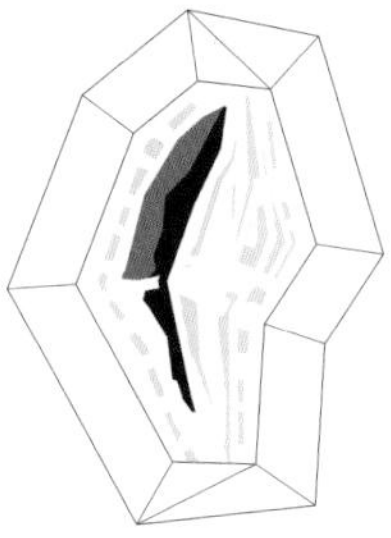

- small herbs/spices/berries
- larger berries/vegetables
- large trees

block diagram

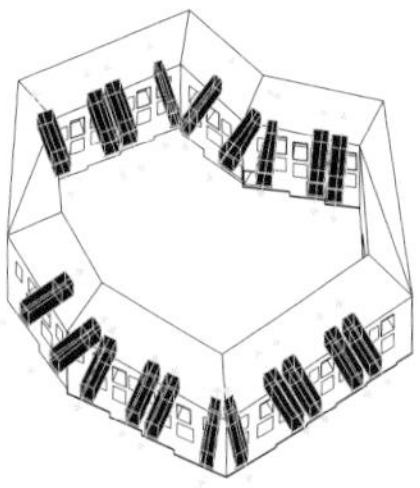

kitchen/dining room

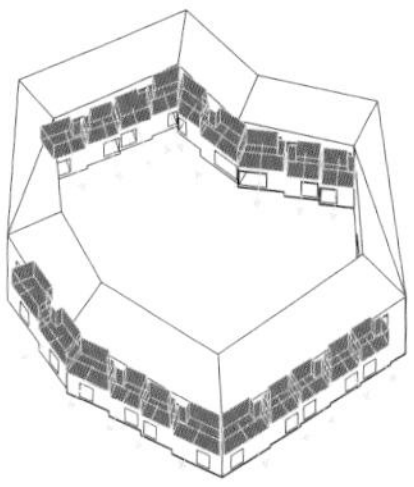

living room

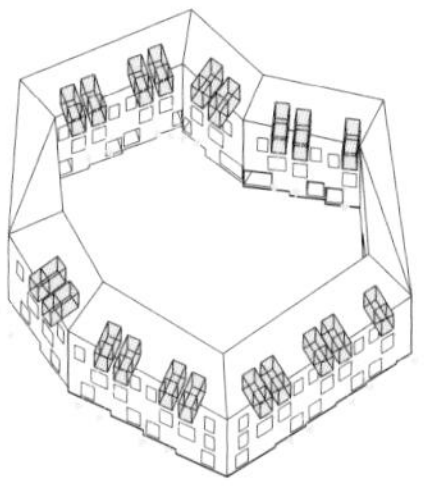

vista room

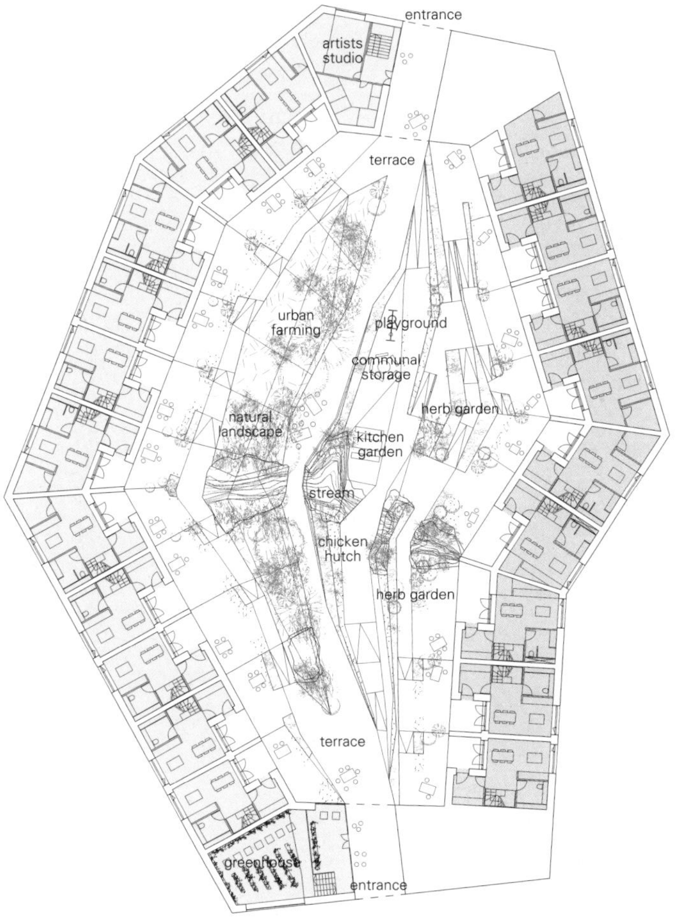
entrance
artists studio
terrace
urban farming
playground
communal storage
herb garden
natural landscape
kitchen garden
stream
chicken hutch
herb garden
terrace
greenhouse
entrance

first floor_cottage 4

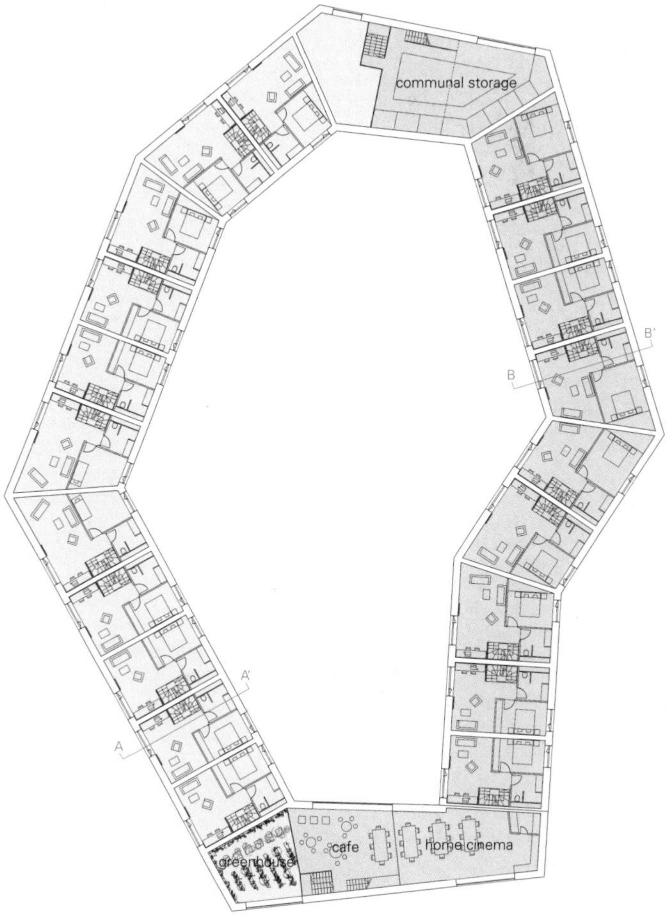
communal storage
B
B'
A
A'
greenhouse
cafe
home cinema

second floor_cottage 4

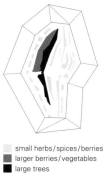

settlement/construction principle

example of ring build-up

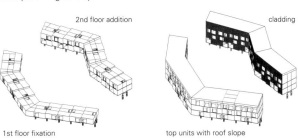

2nd floor addition

1st floor fixation

cladding

top units with roof slope

community spaces & green roof

stream   east elevation _ cottage 4   stream

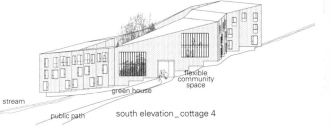

flexible community space

stream   green house

public path   south elevation _ cottage 4

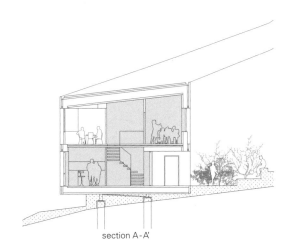

section A-A'

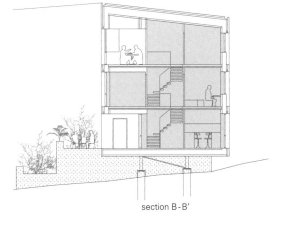

section B-B'

PLOT T10, the Rive Gauche neighbourhood project_Atelier Phileas + LA Architectures + SeARCH

One of the challenges of the Rive Gauche neighbourhood project is to recreate a strong, physical link between the south of the 13th arrondissement and the banks of the Seine. As such, the railway tracks have been recovered and built, with several cross-cutting paths leading between the newly constructed buildings.

The T10A South block has a strategic position in the neighbourhood: it is found at its edge, directly linked to one of Paris' oldest regions. It sits at the end of an extended view down the 400 meter promenade which runs along the Halle Freyssinet building.

The project sits at the intersection between urban routes, railways, an esplanade, and varied building densities, including low density (Halle Freyssinet), high density and framing buildings. Beyond these long reaching views, the facades will be viewed up close, through its use as a living space.

This desire to transform Paris is clear in the developments carried out in the Paris Rive Gauche neighbourhood. Paris wants friendliness, a city with human dimensions which benefits from the height of the buildings in this neighbourhood to open up to the air and sun. A city with light links, accessible on foot and bicycle, but above all an increasingly environmentally-friendly city.

Our concept for the three plots is cross-cutting. Each building has its own architectural identity, but they are all united under several shared ideas.

- The skyline is broken with openings to look through, allowing the air and light to circulate. The angles are chiselled, the buildings streamlined.
- The facades make their role and use as a living space obvious (It is clear that it is housing and student housing) however from a distance the staggered depths gives them a very urban appeal.
- The environment as a key theme: Each resident has a tree within easy reach. Shared terraces and gardens, private planted terraces and loggias, green gardens, green roofs planted with large trees. This biodiversity will be visible everywhere, on our facades and available to residents, students and families, and people working for the SNCF.

- The garden will be visible from afar, in front of the Halle Freyssinet building and at a distance, with two beautiful visual openings.
The garden and the building facades (housing and Minefi) will be illuminated thanks to the broken skyline and openings. The ground floor commercial areas are as transparent as possible. The water extends up to our garden through the use of plants and mirrors.
At the meeting point between the esplanade, water and monumental staircase, we create a visual opening to a garden which means that the garden is not behind the buildings but within the urban landscape.

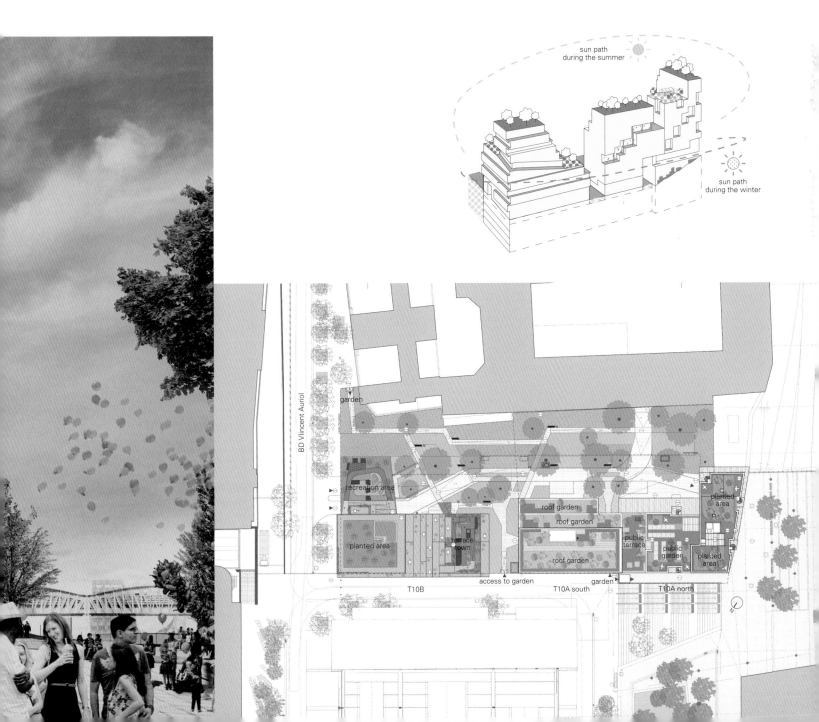

파리 리브 고슈 T10 지구 공동주택

'리브 고슈'는 프랑스 파리 남동부 13구역 안에서도 센 강 서쪽으로 인접한 지역이다. 과거에는 공업 단지였지만 노후화된 이곳을 되살리기 위해 재개발에 착수했고, 1990년 개발 승인을 받은 후 25년이 지난 지금까지도 여전히 개발 중이다.

리브 고슈 지역 개발의 핵심은 13구역과 센 강 사이를 연결하는 것이다. 둘 사이를 가로막던 오래된 철로를 복원하고, 동시에 주변으로 건물이 들어설 땅을 새로 다졌다. 정비된 대지에는 주거시설과 업무시설, 학교, 공원 등이 들어섰고, 앞으로도 지어질 예정이다.

그중 강과 구도심, 철로가 모두 인접해있는 T10 구역은 리브 고슈 지역의 요충지다. 이곳을 개발하기 위해 파리의 주택 공급 및 재개발 사업을 관장하는 파리 해비타트에서 새 주상복합 건물을 계획하는 공모를 열고, 아틀리에 필레아스, LA 아키텍쳐, 서치 팀의 제출안을 당선작으로 선정했다.

대상지는 일상에서 마주하는 길과 산책로, 철도가 교차하는 곳으로, 다양한 높낮이와 밀도의 건물들이 즐비하다. 한때는 철도 차고지로 사용되다 지금은 대규모 복합시설로의 재건축을 앞둔 '프레이시네 홀'을 따라 400m의 기나긴 보행도로를 지나면 그 끝에 건물이 자리한다.

설계안은 일상의 삶과 도시의 주요한 기틀이라는 두 가지 주제를 내세운다. 거주민들의 생활 공간이자 만남의 장소 역할을 하면서, 녹음으

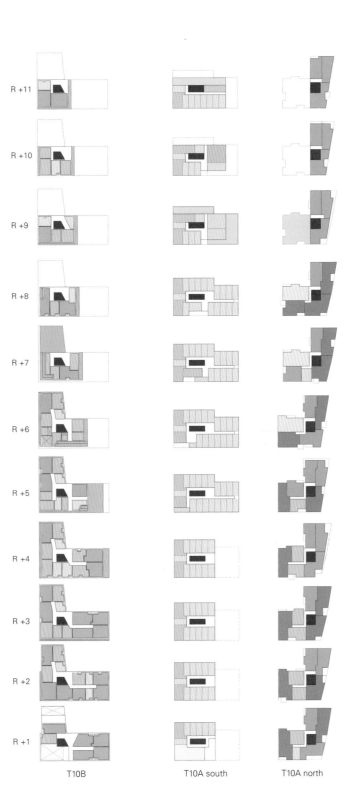

	T10B	T10A south	T10A north
R +11			
R +10			
R +9			
R +8			
R +7			
R +6			
R +5			
R +4			
R +3			
R +2			
R +1			

로 가득한 산책로 같은 건물을 구상했다. 도시에 존재하는 하나의 장소로서 다른 외부 요인들과 관계를 맺기 위해 거주민뿐만 아니라, 시민들도 적극적으로 끌어들였다. 따라서 도보와 자전거로도 진입할 수 있는 환경친화적인 건물을 계획했다.

부지에는 총 세 개의 건물이 들어선다. 설계에 참여한 세 건축 팀이 각각 한 개의 동을 맡았는데, 전체를 아우르는 공통적인 개념을 담으면서도 각자의 고유 성향을 드러냈다. 세 동의 건물은 나란히 붙어있지만 위로 갈수록 좁아지게 설계해 건물 사이 사이에 간격이 생겼다. 덕분에 여느 밀도 높은 공동주택 건물과 달리 내부에 공기와 빛의 순환이 활발하게 이뤄진다. 건물 간의 간격이 여유로워 12층 이상의 규

모임에도 답답하거나 꽉 막혀 보이지 않는다.

건물의 또 다른 주요 개념은 자연이다. 옥상 정원뿐만 아니라 층마다 개인 테라스나 로지아 등의 야외 공간을 두었다. 심지어 건물 중간층은 일부를 비워 공용 테라스와 정원을 만들고 다양한 식물을 심었다. 곳곳에 비워진 공간 사이로 녹음이 무성한 외관은 인근 어디에서나 눈에 띄어 지나가는 이에게 시각적인 아름다움도 선사한다.

건물은 주상복합 시설로, 사회 임대 주택을 포함하여 학생 주거, 일반 주거, 업무, 상업 시설 등으로 구성된다. 상업이나 업무 등 공공시설이 들어선 1층은 투명성을 강조하기 위해 도시를 향해 열려 있다.

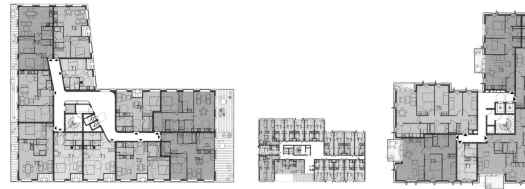

T10B   T10A south   T10A north

ground floor

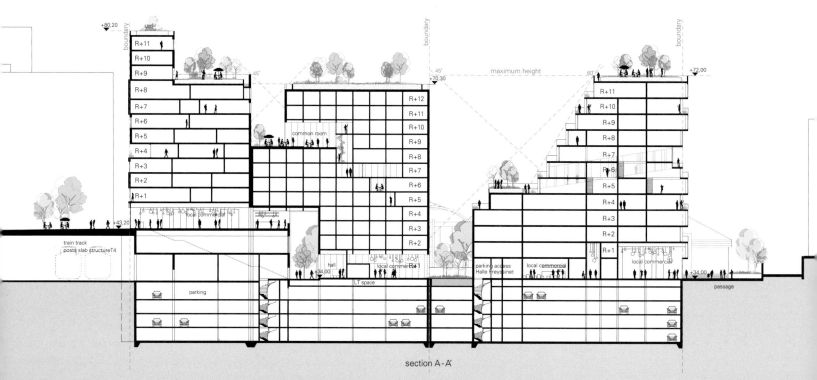

section A - A'

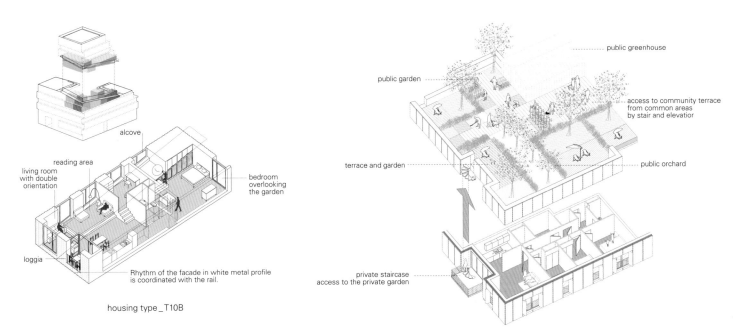

alcove

reading area

living room
with double
orientation

bedroom
overlooking
the garden

loggia

Rhythm of the facade in white metal profile
is coordinated with the rail.

housing type _ T10B

public greenhouse

public garden

access to community terrace
from common areas
by stair and elevation

terrace and garden

public orchard

private staircase
access to the private garden

public + private park _ T10A north

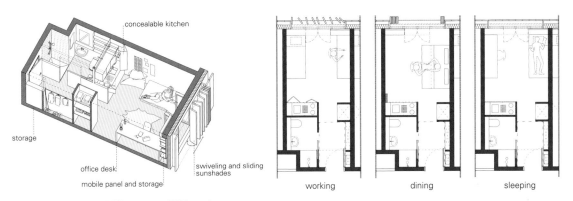

concealable kitchen

storage

office desk

mobile panel and storage

swiveling and sliding
sunshades

housing type and different uses _ T10A south

working   dining   sleeping

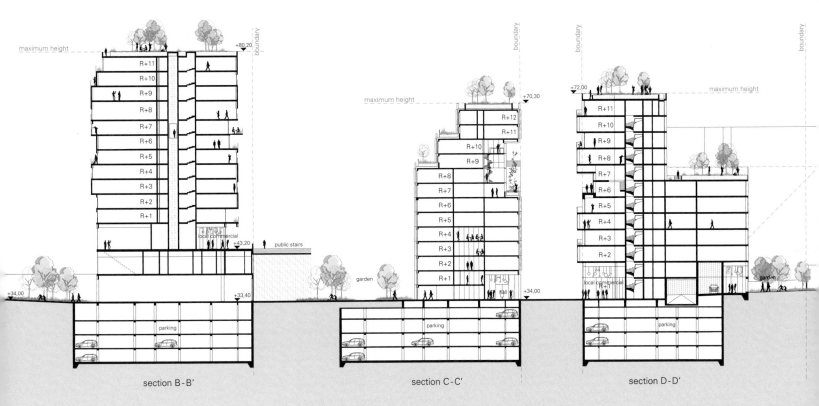

section B - B'

section C - C'

section D - D'

Hybrid Housing in Hamburg "We are here to stay" _Gabriele Filippi

'Hybrid housing' was a conceptual architecture competition hosted by Ctrl + space. The contest's goal was the creation of a single mixed-use (mostly residential) building in Hamburg, Germany. The site, in which a public housing building was demolished, is called "Esso Hauser", located behind the commercial port.

The variety and hybridity are the focus of the project. The building is composed of a seemingly endless variety of routes, places, functions, visual cues, materials, windows, and architectural forms. The conglomeration of all is so complex and unpredictable that it effectively mirrors the chaos of modern life. Private and public are interwoven amongst streets and tangents, breaking the monotony of life, showing inhabitants the beauty of spontaneity.

The volumetric composition of the block provides for a fragmentation of the whole into smaller volumes, to form a mosaic of buildings adjustable in height and depth; the urban image, in the heights and the overall size, is maintained in respect of the alignments of the historic fabric, but at the same time principle of variety is introduced and promoted:

the fragmentation of the block in individual flanked buildings breaks the monotony and the heaviness of a too large and trivial block.

The ground is open to the city, a place for the city and for the citizens. The project seeks to embody the spirit of the place of St. Pauli, a fight, rebel, unconventional neighborhood. Being clearly an architectural response to all recent history of the location and the city, the different elements that constitute the whole complex are reactive of the urban surroundings, whether in scale or configuration. The hybridity of the build-

ing comes from all the bridges established with the city fabric, either concrete or metaphorical; the building is open and accessible to the generality of public in all its public spaces. Structure takes here an important presence, the exoskeleton enforces the unfinished quality of the space, apart from introducing a strong graphical appeal. Harnessing the qualities of its environment and gathering the essential ingredients of the city, this project constitutes a city within the city, permeable to the outside, providing a framework to urban activities, placemaking as a process and a underlining philosophy".

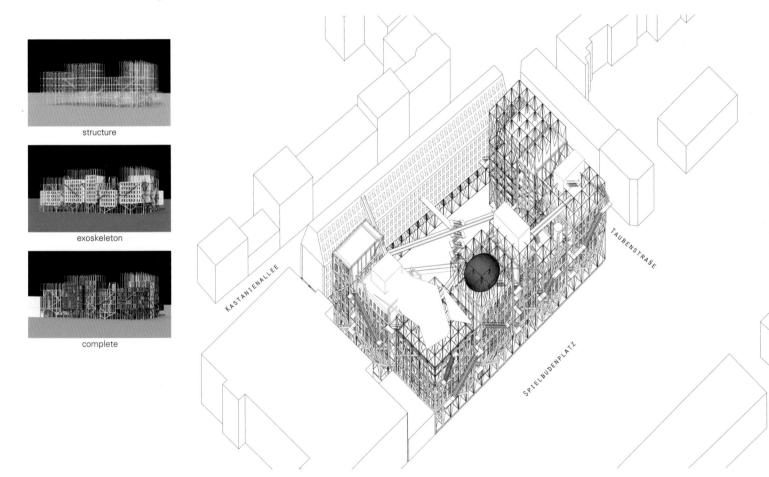

structure

exoskeleton

complete

KASTANIENALLEE

TAUBENSTRAßE

SPIELBUDENPLATZ

함부르크 공동주택, '여기 살리라'

독일 함부르크 시의 주상복합 설계 경기 당선작으로 '여기 살리라'가 선정됐다. 함부르크 항구 바로 앞 부지에 원래 있던 공동주택 건물은 이미 철거된 상태였다. 당선작은 다양한 요소들이 한데 아우러지고 뒤섞인 '복합체'를 주요 개념으로 삼았다. 건물은 여러 재료를 사용해 다양한 공간 형태를 이룬다. 수없이 만들어진 복잡한 길과 장소가 경관을 만들어내며 마치 오늘날의 혼돈을 반영하는 듯하다. 사적인 공간과 공적인 공간은 때로는 길을 따라 뒤섞인다. 건물은 단조로움에서 벗어나 복합체로서의 아름다움을 드러낸다.

작은 형태들로 파편화된 건물은 마치 모자이크처럼 적정한 높이와 깊이의 전체를 이룬다. 각 건물은 더 작은 공간들로 쪼개어지면서 더는 묵직하거나 단조롭지 않다. 이렇게 만들어진 다양한 공간들은 역사적

인 도시 풍경에 규모를 맞춰 자리잡는다.

한편, 1층은 시민들을 위한 공공장소로 열려 마치 광장처럼 쓰인다. 부지와 도시가 지금까지 지녀왔던 모든 역사적 맥락에 건축적으로 명확하게 대응하고, 도시의 규모에 맞게 반응한다. 건물 내부에는 각 공간을 잇는 다리를 두어 서로 어우러지는 공간적 특성을 취한다. 때문에 공간의 구조 체계는 매우 중요하다. 외부에 노출된 골조들은 강렬한 시각적 효과를 줄 뿐만 아니라, 아직도 건물이 지어지고 있는 듯한 인상을 주기도 한다.

이렇게 계획된 건물은 주변 도시의 요소들을 끌어들이며, 도시 안에 새로운 도시를 만든다. 밖을 향해 열려 도시의 다양한 활동을 위한 틀이 되는 동시에, 독특한 건축적 관념을 담은 채 시민 모두가 함께할 수 있는 장소를 마련해준다.

south-east elevation

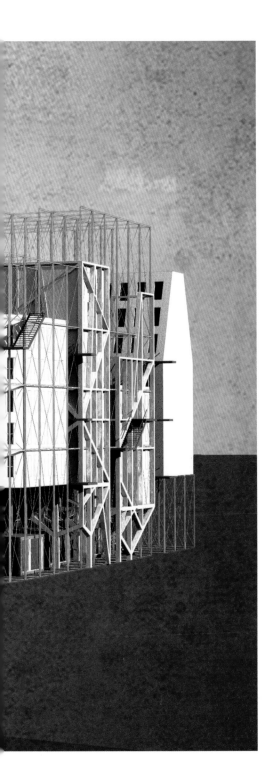

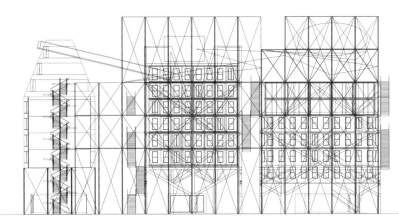

north-east elevation

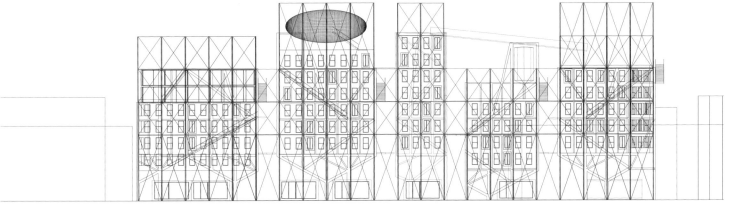

north-west elevation

ground floor

collectives functions floor

roof

Modern Vernacular

Bridging Traditio Innovatio

All architecture reproduces, adopts, and adapts precedents to a greater or lesser extent. After all, none of us grows up or lives in a vacuum. If not always consciously, our built environment affects us on a subliminal, unconscious level. It is the role of architects to react to and interpret their built environment and hopefully, to improve it. The gulf between avant-garde grand gestures of many contemporary buildings and the twee nostalgia of buildings that are designed to be "in-keeping" with historic traditions might seem unbridgeable. The boundary between authentic design and second-rate pastiche is often unclear. How can architects today reconcile these two seemingly irreconcilable approaches into one cohesive approach? Some architects are not dismissive of past precedents, but rather see the legitimacy and "hard-won knowledge" inherent in vernacular buildings and incorporate traditional ideas and construction methods into their work. These architects display the capacity to overcome the dichotomy between drawing knowledge and expertise from the past and creating work that is true to the zeitgeist of the twenty-first century.

크건 작건 모든 건축물은 선례를 받아들이고, 때론 고치며, 심지어 다시 만들기도 한다. 외부와 단절된 곳에서 사는 사람은 없기에, 주변 환경은 부지불식간에 우리에게 영향을 미치게 마련이다. 그래서 건축 환경을 해석하고, 반응하며, 나아가 개선하는 것이 바라건대 건축가의 역할일 것이다.

전위적이고 화려한 몸짓을 뽐내는 현대 건축과 역사와 전통의 향수를 간직한 건축 사이의 격차는 좁히기 어려워 보인다. 진짜와 아류의 경계 역시 모호하다. 오늘날의 건축가들이 어떻게 하면 이 두 가지 접근 방식을 하나로 통합할 수 있을까? 토속 건축이 내재한 정통성을 무시하지 않고, 이를 연구해 얻은 전통 아이디어와 시공법을 자신의 작업과 접목하는 건축가들이 있다. 이들은 과거에서부터 전해 내려온 지식, 전문성과 21세기 시대정신에 부합하는 창작 사이의 한계를 극복하는 역량을 보여준다.

n and
n

전통과 혁신

In our copy-paste era, when built environments the world over have the same ubiquitous accumulation of high rise buildings and generic shopping malls, it is refreshing to see that there are architects who still believe in the importance of creating architecture that realizes an identity with values and images that are locally cultivated, whilst also reflecting contemporary technology, materials, and ideas. Not an architectural style per se, but an approach to design that reconciles what might at first seem irreconcilable.

For this issue, C3 has selected a collection of projects by various architectural practices from three continents to illustrate the variety of ways in which architects from around the world re-interpret regional building practices and vernacular styles in a modern context. It will be shown how they reinterpret the use of materials, construction methods, and details in new, innovative ways and how they have the capacity to steer architecture away from slavish trendsetting and avoid reducing architecture to a form of high fashion.

흔하디흔한 복사-불이기의 시대에 사는 우리는 전 세계 어딜 가도 비슷비슷한 고층 건물과 쇼핑몰 건물을 만난다. 그렇기에 현대 과학 기술과 소재를 반영해 아이디어를 생산해 내면서도, 지역색이 지닌 가치와 이미지로 정체성을 실현할 수 있다고 믿는 건축가들이 있다는 것은 주목할 만하다. 이것은 건축 양식에 대한 이야기가 아니다. 처음에는 양립할 수 없어 보이던 것을 조화롭게 만드는 디자인 접근법에 대한 이야기다.

이번 호에서 C3는 세계 각지의 건축가들이 현지 건축의 관례와 토속 양식을 현대적 맥락으로 재해석해내는 다양한 방식들을 소개하기 위해 각기 다른 대륙에 자리한 다섯 개의 건축물을 선정했다. 건축가들이 어떻게 건축을 최신 유행의 수단으로만 삼지 않으면서 맹목적인 유행 추구와 거리를 두고 작업했는지, 현지의 자재, 공법, 디테일을 어떻게 새롭고 혁신적으로 재해석했는지 자세히 살펴보고자 한자.

©Marc Ryckaert

The Mosque at New Gourna, Luxor, Egypt, 1946, Hassan Fathy

Modern Vernacular - Bridging Tradition and Innovation

Within the term "modern vernacular", there is an interesting paradox. If we take each term as an entity and unpack its meaning, the paradox is elucidated. While the term "vernacular," as its etymology suggests, incorporates notions like "indigenous, domestic, native," the opposite "contempory" and "international" are inherent in the word "modern." Vernacular architecture is an expansive, grassroots concept encompassing culture, climate, craft, and myth, as opposed to modern architecture, which is scientific, technical, rational, and universal. Where vernacular architecture is anonymous, unselfconscious, and based on repetition, modern architecture has an architect as design author, is self-aware, and is concerned with questions of style. Vernacular buildings are built by local craftspeople with cheap and abundant materials from the region; whilst modern buildings are designed by architects for their clients with materials that are not necessarily locally sourced. Vernacular architecture evolved over centuries in specific contexts and climates for specific cultural communities, whilst modern architecture grew out of the ruins of post-War Europe in the ateliers of individual theorist architects, like Le Corbusier and Walter Gropius.

It could be said that the post-War success of modernism smothered regional developments in architecture, cloaking the world in a ubiquitous sheath of buildings with little or no relationship to their specific contexts. For a long period regional architecture was dismissed by the intellectual elite, as architects abandoned their cultural past in order to embrace modern civilization. After the Second World War, architects understandably sought to rid their designs from overt cultural references and signs of national identity. Modernism suited this ethos; its low-budget technology was a quick-fix solution to a post-war housing crisis. Running contrary to the endemic spread of modernism was also a reawakening to the riches and charm of regional design and architecture. The rootedness, sense of identity, and belonging that vernacular architecture engendered was recognized. As a response, vari-

현대적 토속 – 전통과 혁신을 잇다

현대적 토속이라는 말은 흥미로운 역설을 담고 있다. '토속'은 말 그대로, '원산, 국내, 토종'과 같은 개념들을 포함하는데, '동시대적', '국제적'이라는 의미가 내재한 '현대'라는 단어와 반대된다. 토속 건축은 문화, 기후, 기술, 신화를 포함하는 포괄적이고 민속적인 특징을 담고 있어, 과학적, 기술적, 이성적, 세계적인 현대 건축과 반대된다. 토속 건축이 특정 작자가 없으며, 무의식적이고, 반복에 근거한다면, 현대 건축은 건축가가 존재하며, 자각적이고, 양식 문제에 민감하다. 토속 건물은 현지 장인들이 그 지역에서 난 풍부하고 저렴한 자재로 짓지만, 현대 건물은 건축가가 건축주를 위해 설계하고, 꼭 현지산일 필요는 없는 자재들이 사용된다. 토속 건축은 특정 지역의 맥락과 기후를 가진 문화 공동체를 위해 수세기에 걸쳐 진화된 것이고, 현대 건축은 2차 세계대전 후 유럽의 폐허 속에서 르코르뷔지에와 발터 그로피우스와 같은 개인 사상가의 작업실에서 나와 발전한 것이다.

전후 모더니즘의 성공으로 인해 세계 각지의 건물들은 지리적 맥락과는 관계없는 유비쿼터스라는 외피를 두르게 되었는데, 이것이 지역 건축과 그 발전을 말살시켰다고 보는 것도 무리가 아니다. 오랫동안 지역 건축은 지적 엘리트층에 의해 묵살되었고, 건축가들도 근대 문명을 수용하기 위해 문화의 과거를 버렸다. 2차 세계대전이 끝난 후, 건축가들은 주택 대란을 해소하기 위해 기능과 효용을 기반으로 한 모더니즘에 탐닉하는 동시에, 자신의 디자인에서 문화적 요소나 지역의 정체성을 나타내는 표식들 또한 당연한 듯 제거해냈다.

하지만 모더니즘의 지역 확산에 반하는 움직임은 부유층을 환기했고, 다시금 지역적 디자인과 건축의 매력을 되돌아보게 해주었다. 토속 건축이 근원에 대한 인식과 정체성, 소속성을 불러일으킨 것이다. 그 응답으로, 많은 현대 건축가들이 자신의 디자인에 지역 토착성의 풍미를 가득 채움으로써 과거에 경의를 표했다. 이집트 건축가 하산 화티는

Marie Short, 1974-75 / Glenn Murcutt House, 1980; Kempsey, Australia, Glenn Murcutt

©Anthony Browell (courtesy of Architecture Foundation Australia

Church mortuary, Vrin, 2003, Gion A. Caminada

©Adrian Michael

ous architects from countries across the world paid tribute to techniques of the past by imbuing their contemporary design with the flavor of local vernacular. Architects like Hassan Fathy in Egypt, who studied Nubian settlements incorporating their technology into his tactile mud-brick vaults, or Geoffrey Bawa whose courtyard houses in South East Asia blur interior and exterior spaces in lush tropical gardens, veteran Mexican architect, Luis Barragan, whose richly-colored houses are rooted in the architect's personal memories of pueblos, Gawie Fagan who employed sculptural forms for his regionalist houses in South Africa, or Glenn Murcutt whose delicate corrugated houses in Australia won him the Pritzker Prize. Swiss architect, Gion A. Caminada, is another important protagonist of modern vernacular. He believes in the importance of building in close proximity to his local community with materials and skills drawn from nearby, embracing humble and ordinary forms situated modestly within their rural contexts. His buildings are so subtle that they hardly draw any attention to themselves.

누비아 주거지에서 현지 기술을 도입해 진흙 벽돌 볼트를 만들었고, 스리랑카의 제프리 바와는 동남아시아의 중정형 주택에서 우거진 열대 정원으로 실내외의 경계를 허물었다. 멕시코 건축가 루이스 바라간의 화려한 색채의 주택들은 인디언 토속 주택에 대한 건축가의 개인적 향수에 근원을 두고 있다. 고위 패간은 남아프리카의 지역주의에 맞는 조형적 형태의 주택을 설계하였으며, 프리츠커 수상자인 호주 건축가 글렌 멀컷은 자연 친화적이며 지역색을 갖춘 주택 작품을 두루 선보였다. 스위스 건축가 지온 A. 카미나다 역시 또 한명의 현대적 토속 건축의 주역이다. 그는 건축의 중요성이 지역 공동체와의 긴밀한 유대와 인접 지역에서 끌어온 자재와 인력에 있으며, 지역적 맥락 안에 소박하게 자리 잡고 있는 평범한 건축물을 함께 품는 데 있다고 믿는다. 그의 건물들은 눈에 띄게 도드라지지 않게 조용히 자리한다. C3가 엄선한 작품들은 멕시코, 태국, 중국, 모로코, 미국에 이르기까지 여러 대륙에 걸쳐 자리한다. 모두 각 지역의 특색에 맞는 '토속적'

From the wealth of buildings across the globe, C3 has earmarked a few buildings from various far-flung countries, like Morocco, America, China, and Thailand, to highlight the most recent examples of modern vernacular architecture. Each of these projects will be briefly analyzed and investigated for its "modern vernacular" credentials.

The renowned Japanese architect, Tadao Ando, reinterprets the spirit of traditional Japanese architecture in his concrete architecture. In his Bosco Studio & House on Mexico's Pacific Ocean, Ando has skillfully woven together the traditional dried palm leave roofscapes of Mexico's palapa pavilions with his trademark use of off-shutter concrete. The shaggy hip roofs sharply contrast with the cool, smooth concrete surfaces. By combining local traditional materials with the abstract, dispassionate concrete—a somewhat incongruous juxtaposition—Ando has created a complex that is both rooted in the specific Mexican landscape, while also connected to a universal language of contemporary architecture.

요소를 '현대적'으로 가미했다. 우리는 각 건축물에 대해 간략하게 분석하고 현대적 토속성의 요건을 살펴보고자 한다.

정갈한 콘크리트 건축으로 잘 알려진 일본 건축가 안도 다다오는 멕시코 전통 건축의 정신을 그만의 방식으로 풀어냈다. 남태평양을 정면으로 마주한 멕시코 오악사카 주의 해변에 예술가를 위한 스튜디오 겸 주택이 들어섰다. 안도는 말린 야자나무 잎으로 만든 멕시코 전통의 팔라파 지붕을 재현하고, 자신의 건축 상징인 노출 콘크리트와 조화시켰다. 초가지붕을 연상케 하는 덥수룩한 지붕은 차갑고 정갈한 콘크리트와는 사뭇 다른 분위기를 자아낸다. 투박한 지역산 전통 소재와 모더니즘을 대표하는 콘크리트를 접목함으로써 멕시코 특유의 환경에 근간을 두면서도 현대 건축의 표본으로 복합적인 면모를 동시에 일궈낸다. 다음으로 미로 리베라 아키텍츠가 미국 오스틴에 설계한 친마야 힌두

Bosco Studio & House, Mexico

Chinmaya Mission Austin by Miro Rivera Architects in neighboring America is another building where the roof forms dominate the architecture. A Hindu temple in Austin, Texas might seem like a slightly bizarre juxtaposition and a tricky brief for which to find appropriate architectural forms. For their design for the Hindu mission, Miro Rivera sought to reinterpret traditional Indian typologies in a modern, Western context. The architects applied their knowledge of local building materials and construction techniques to create a visual language that is richly textured and sculptural in form. Low-slung hipped roofs and white stucco walls are reminiscent of traditional Hindu buildings in India. Deep eaves offer refuge from the harsh Texan sun. The northeast facing, square temple structure is adorned with a dramatic crown, like a feather-comb that demarcates the spiritual heart of the complex. Playing with strict symmetry, the mandala-like plan of concentric circles, squares, and rectangles and the illuminated petal-shape suspended off the ceiling are all reminders of traditional Hindu temples. With the temple at its core, the plan progresses outward from the central meditation hall and moves out toward the perimeter boundary made from vertical blocks of locally sourced limestone. Color is a vital ingredient in Hindu buildings, here the color scheme is rather muted, the only saturated color is the deep spicy ochre on the curved inner temple wall. Situated perpendicular to one another, the two complex structures create an open square of verdant lawn where one can imagine Hindu monks meditating or practicing yoga at sunrise. Though so geographically far from India, this Hindu complex creates a subtle proximity to the spirit of Asian Hinduism.

Fan Zeng Art Gallery in Nantong, China is another poignant example of contemporary vernacular architecture. Original Design Studio was inspired by vernacular Chinese forms for their museum, which is dedicated to the Chinese master calligrapher, artist, and poet, Fan Zeng. Traditional Chinese pagoda buildings are frequently raised on stone bases and surrounded by ponds of water as was prescribed by cosmological concepts in traditional Chinese architecture, like

교 사원을 살펴보자. 앞선 멕시코 스튜디오 사례와 마찬가지로 지붕 형태가 무엇보다 인상적이지만, 전혀 다른 뉘앙스를 풍긴다. 이 건물은 신앙생활을 위한 힌두교 사원이기에 보편적인 사원의 공간 구성을 지키면서 현대적인 새로움을 더한다. 기하학 형태로 대칭성이 드러나는 전통 사원과는 달리, 두 동의 건물이 기역 자로 놓이는 다소 특이한 병렬 구조를 지닌다. 그로 인해 두 건물 사이로 현대에서 흔히 찾아볼 수 있는 중정형 마당이 생겨났다. 열린 마당에서 수도승들이 명상하거나 요가를 수행하는 모습도 볼 수 있다. 건축가는 풍부한 재질감과 조각적인 형태를 지닌 예스러운 모습을 만들어내기 위해 지역산 건축 자재를 사용하여 자신만의 시공법을 구축했다. 추녀마루를 낮춰 납작하게 만든 지붕과 새하얀 스타코 마감의 벽은 인도의 전통 힌두교 건물을 연상시킨다. 낮지만 깊은 처마는 텍사스의 강한 햇빛을 가려주는 그늘막이 된다. 이와는 대조적으로 북동쪽에 놓인 정사각형 예배당 건물은 상당히 경사진 지붕 위로 왕관을 쓴 듯 우뚝 솟은 첨탑이 인상적이다. 천정의 첨탑을 따라 하늘로 이어지는 흐름은 이 예배 공간이 영적인 중심부임을 드러낸다. 이 안에 담긴 엄격한 대칭 구도와 전통 문양인 '만다라'를 빗댄 조명, 중앙에 무게를 둔 평면, 천장에 매달린 꽃잎 형태가 모두 전통 힌두 양식을 적용했다. 힌두교 사원에서 화려한 색감은 가장 필수적인 요소인데 반해, 이 건물에는 다소 차분한 색채 배합이 이뤄진다. 유일하게 높은 채도의 황토색만이 내부 휘어진 벽면에 입혀져 공간의 분위기를 자아낸다. 이처럼 인도 고유의 신앙인 힌두교 사원은 비록 인도와는 무관한 타지에서, 현대의 모습으로 변모했지만, 그 전통성을 계승하여 정신만은 동양 세계에 근접해있다. 앞선 사례들은 전통 지붕 형태를 취하거나 보편적인 사원의 공간 배치를 적용하는 등 토속적인 성향과 전통성을 물리적인 형태로 설명했다. 다음에 소개할 오리지날 디자인 스튜디오의 범증 미술관은 이와는 조금 다른 시각으로 전통과 현대, 두 세계를 연결한다. 중국 난퉁에 자리한 이 박물관은 중국의 거장 예술가이자 서예가, 그리고 시인인 범증

Fan Zeng Art Gallery, China

feng shui. Original Design Studio has incorporated these aspects into their gallery design. Resting on a cut stone base, delicately perforated in a gesture of a wave, the museum is rather like a translucent lantern in an open field, alluring and mystical. When the sun warms the pools of water surrounding the building, it seems to hover like an apparition in the mists. By reflecting sunlight and mirroring the subtle colors of the sky, the building becomes intricately tied to its site, like the pigments in a watercolor painting. Planned around an interior courtyard, the building echoes classical Chinese architecture where interior courtyards were used to regulate temperatures and ventilate spaces. Gently perched above shimmering screen-like facades, the calligraphic form of the roof is a subtle reinterpretation of the roof typology of traditional Chinese courtyard houses—it is also a pertinent form to represent Fan Zeng's art. On the fiftieth anniversary of the Cultural Revolution in China, it is refreshing to see a contemporary building that embraces the beautiful forms and symbols of traditional Chinese architecture, rather than the importation of culturally generic forms that simply ignore local culture, climate, and context.

Studiomake claim that they rarely start their design process with iconographic or symbolic forms, though their design for Guan Yin Pavilion for the Chinese-Thai Institute at Rangsit University in Thailand is an exception. Architecture plays a major role in Thailand's cultural legacy and reflects both the challenges of living in Thailand's extremely humid climate as well as, historically, the importance of architecture to the Thai people's sense of community and religious beliefs. The question for the architects was how to express inter-cultural and academic dialogue between China and Thailand in an appropriate architectural language that was somehow infused with both cultures. Studiomake employed both form, material, and color to convey the transnational interchange that the building should foster. The elegant roof form dominates the building and is loosely based on a traditional sala or an open pavilion used as a meeting place and to protect people from sun and rain, and which are generally open on all four

을 위한 곳으로 유물과도 같은 그의 작품 컬렉션을 만날 수 있다. 역사적인 인물을 기리는 건물인 만큼 중국 특유의 토속 건축에서 영감을 얻었다. 우주 철학에서 비롯된 건축 개념의 대표적인 원리인 풍수지리에 따라 중국 전통의 사탑은 대부분 초석 위에 건물을 세우고 연못에 둘러싸인다. 이를 바탕으로 건물은 전통적인 요소를 현대식으로 재현했다. 다듬어진 돌 사이로 섬세하게 구멍을 낸 벽은 건물을 지탱하는 기단부가 되고, 그 위로는 반투명 랜턴처럼 신비롭게 빛난다. 또한, 건물을 에워싼 연못은 햇빛에 데워지면 안개가 자욱해 마치 유령이 떠도는 듯 몽롱하다. 건물은 태양 빛을 투영시켜 하늘의 미묘한 색감을 입은 채 부지 안에서 한 폭의 수채화 그림이 된다. 동양의 건축에서 가장 중요하게 여기는 자연과의 관계를 명확히 드러내고 있다. 스크린처럼 내부가 비치는 외벽 위로 얹혀진 지붕은 중국 전통의 중정 주택의 지붕을 재해석한 것이다. 서예 하듯 물결치는 형태의 지붕은 범증의 예술을 표현하기에도 적절하다. 건물의 내부 중정 역시, 기온을 조절하고 환기를 시키는 중국식 전통 마당이 반영되었다. 올해로 중국 문화 대혁명의 50주년을 맞아 지역 문화, 기후, 맥락 등을 무시하는 천편일률적인 형태가 아닌, 전통의 아름다움과 상징을 동시에 아우르는 현대적인 건물을 짓고자 했다.

스튜디오메이크가 설계한 태국 랑싯 대학교의 관인 파빌리온은 중국과 태국의 문화 교류를 위한 건물이다. 태국의 문화유산에서 건축은 중요한 역할을 한다. 극도로 습한 기후에서 비롯된 일상의 어려움, 역사적으로 태국인이 가지는 공동체 의식과 종교적 믿음을 모두 반영해야 하기 때문이다. 중국과 태국 사이의 이문화적이고 학문적 대화를 두 문화가 서로에게 어떤 식으로든 스며들 수 있는 적절한 건축언어를 사용하여 표현하는 것이 건축가들의 가장 큰 고민이었다. 스튜디오메이크는 두 국가 사이의 교류를 상징하고자 형태, 재료, 색채를 모두 고려했다. 건물은 태국 전통의 '살라', 즉 개방형 파빌리온 위에 지붕을 얹은 형식으로 설계됐다. 건축가는 태국 전통 건축의 뾰족한 지붕 형

Casa-Port Railway Station, Morocco
©Didier Boy de La Tour

sides. Here, two volumes, linked by an open air courtyard are covered by a single, sweeping concrete roof that rises in the center like the spine of an open book, or the wings of a bird. The roof form imparts the building with an exotic flavor of traditional Thai architecture. Studiomake has not merely mimicked the peaked forms of local Thai roof morphology, but have reinterpreted them. Materiality is central to Studio-make's architecture. By firing the bricks twice, the clay bricks turn from red to grey. Thus the building is constructed from red Thai earth that is transformed to the traditional grey of Chinese masonry, an apt metaphor for a Chinese-Thai Institute. The bricks have been molded, like wavelets that echo the form of the roof at a small scale. Masonry has been used in two ways: on one side of the building, it has been left perforated, creating an undulating screen-like wall, while on the other they from a solid, deep grey wall. Like Fan Zeng Gallery, water is an integral to the design, with reflective ponds surrounding the pavilion building.

The final project in this series of modern vernacular buildings is Casa-Port Railway Station in Casablanca, Morocco by AREP, which is situated at the intersection of the medina, the art deco district, and the contemporary developments of the city center. The station consists of a delicate raised roof held aloft by a forest of slender concrete columns that divide into eight branches at the apex. Perched above each "capital" is a sky-light which filters sunlight down into the concourse. The grid matrix of columns and gently undulating roof create a beautiful timber canopy that shelters the concourse ten meters below. Intricate patterned geometry has played a central role in the art and architecture of Islam for centuries. Traditional mashrabiyya latticework has been employed since the Middle Ages in Islamic buildings as an architectural mechanism to create privacy, filter light, and allow air ventilation to cool interior spaces from the intense desert heat. The perforated screens are created by beautiful interwoven patterns that are an artistic symbiosis of form and function. AREP have cleverly reinterpreted the mashrabiyya using fiber-reinforced concrete in this large public building to screen direct light and views

태를 단지 흉내 낸 것만이 아니라 철저히 재해석했다. 야외 정원으로 연결된 두 개의 볼륨은 펼쳐진 책의 등처럼, 혹은 새의 양 날개처럼 가운데가 솟아올라 있는 하나의 커다란 콘크리트 지붕으로 덮여 있다. 우아한 곡선 지붕은 태국의 뜨거운 빛과 잦은 호우를 피할 수 있다. 건물은 사면이 모두 열려 있어 만남의 장소로 사용되기도 한다. 스튜디오메이크 건축의 핵심 요소는 재료다. 중국과 태국의 교류 상징을 다름 아닌 재료로 나타냈다. 점토 벽돌을 두 번 구우면 붉은색에서 회색으로 변하는데, 이 속성을 이용해 태국의 붉은 점토를 중국 전통 석조 건축의 회색 벽돌로 변신시켰다. 벽돌은 지붕의 솟은 곡선 모양을 작은 스케일로 형상화한 잔물결 무늬로 만들었다. 벽돌은 두 가지 방식으로 쌓았다. 건물의 한쪽 면은 구멍이 뚫린 채로 출렁이는 장막처럼 만들고, 또 다른 면은 단단한 진회색 벽으로 두었다. 또 한 가지 독특한 점은 파빌리온이 연못 한가운데 떠 있다는 점이다. 홍수와 같은 태국의 자연재해에 대응하기 위해 벽과 슬래브는 연못 위에 뜰 수

있는 재료로 만들었다.

마지막 작품은 AREP이 설계한 까사 포트 기차역이다. 모로코 카사 블랑카의 이슬람 구시가지 교차로에 자리한 이 기차역은 가느다란 콘크리트 기둥 숲으로 지붕을 들어 올렸다. 끝을 여덟 가닥의 가지로 나눈 기둥머리 위로 채광창을 내어 중앙 홀로 햇살을 투과시킨다. 완만한 물결모양의 지붕은 아름다운 목제 캐노피가 되어 10m 아래의 중앙 홀을 비바람으로부터 보호한다. 수 세기 동안 복잡한 패턴의 기하학은 이슬람 예술과 건축에서 중요한 역할을 해왔다. 전통 목조 격자 세공 방식을 일컫는 '마쉬라비아'는 중세시대 이슬람 건축에서 사생활을 보호하고, 빛을 적절히 받아들이며, 사막의 강한 열기로부터 실내 공간을 서늘하게 환기하기 위한 건축적 메커니즘으로 사용되었다. 아름다운 패턴으로 엮은 구멍이 뚫린 장막에는 형태와 기능이 예술적으로 공생한다. AREP은 이 마쉬라비아를 영리하게 재해석해 만든 섬유 보강콘크리트를 이 거대한 기차역의 외벽에 사용했다. 직사광선을 차

Guan Yin Pavilion, Thailand
©Spaceshift Studio

into the interior. With their volumes, materials, lighting, and geometric patterns, the station design pays tribute to the heritage of Moroccan palaces and public buildings while at the same time acknowledging modernity.

Modern vernacular encompasses a broad variety of architectural styles from all over the world. As we have seen, many countries have their own proponents of this multidimensional approach to architecture. At a time where seemingly every high street, whether Paris, Rome, New York, or Sydney has the same chain stores housed in similar, glossy buildings, it is important to have a counter movement where specific contexts and historical forms are scrutinized and where knowledge assembled from the past is not only acknowledged, but also reincorporated. In our overpopulated world, where people often feel dehumanized and insignificant, an architecture that references past vernacular and rehumanizes architecture surely has an important role to play. As millions of people are on the move globally, pressure mounts to find intelligent,

economic ways to design and construct buildings that go beyond sleek, good-looking buildings. Modern vernacular poses a resistance to the superficiality of seemingly random, stylistic architecture.

The choice of this years Pritzker prize-winning architect, radical Chilean architect, Alejandro Aravena, who is known for his visionary social housing projects in Latin America, is symptomatic of a shift of values. Pritzker judges maintained that Aravena "epitomises the revival of a more socially engaged architect" giving the profession "a new dimension". Perhaps some of the answers to the pressing needs of architecture today can be found in an approach to design that is hybrid, inclusive, and affordable. Design that incorporates both high-tech and low-tech, grand ideas and pragmatism, universality and belonging, buildings that are both modern and vernacular, giving us the best of both worlds and more humane architecture. Anna Roos

단하면서 내부 공간과 동선도 잘 들여다보이도록 만들었다. 까사 포트 기차역은 형태, 자재, 조명, 기하학적 무늬들을 통해 모로코의 문화유산과 전통에 경의를 표하는 동시에 현대성을 받아들여 잘 어우러낸 사례다.

현대적 토속은 전 세계에 걸쳐 갖가지 건축 양식을 망라한다. 많은 나라가 건축에 대한 자신만의 독특하고도 다차원적인 접근 방식을 갖는다. 파리, 로마, 뉴욕, 시드니 등 여느 대도시의 변화한 중심가에는 비슷비슷하고 화려한 건물과 쌍둥이 같은 체인점들이 즐비해 있다. 반대로 특정 지역의 맥락에 뿌리박은 역사적 건물들을 면밀히 살피고, 과거로부터 축적된 지식을 인정하고 재통합하려는 움직임 또한 중요하다. 인간에 대한 존엄이 하락하는 과잉 인구 시대에, 과거의 토속을 참고하고 인간성을 회복하는 것은 분명 건축에 주어진 중요한 역할이다. 수백만의 인구가 세계 각지를 오가며 분주히 움직이는 가운데, 매끈하

고 보기 좋은 건물을 넘어, 가장 경제적인 디자인과 시공법을 찾는 것이 지상 목표인 시대다. 현대적 토속은 무작위적이고 양식화된 건축의 얄팍함에 문제를 제기한다.

건축의 가치가 차츰 변하고 있다. 라틴 아메리카의 공공 주택 프로젝트로 유명한 칠레의 급진주의적 건축가 알레한드로 아라베나가 올해 프리츠커 상의 수상자로 선정된 것도 이러한 변화와 궤를 함께 한다. 프리츠커상 심사위원들은 아라베나에 대해 '적극적인 사회 참여형 건축가로서 건축계에 새로운 국면을 열어줬다'고 평가했다. 오늘날 건축이 절실히 필요로 하는 것은 융합과 통합, 그리고 합리적이면서도 경쟁력 있는 디자인 접근법이다. 하이테크와 로우테크, 아이디어와 실용, 보편성과 개인성, 현대적이면서도 토속적인 양극단의 특징을 잘 접목한 건축물이야말로 인류의 미래 건축에 대한 해답이 될 수 있을 것이다. 아나 로스

Bosco Studio & House

Tadao Ando Architect & Associates

The project takes place in Puerto Escondido in the Mexican state of Oaxaca. Puerto Escondido is not only known to have one of the best waves in the world for surfing but also known to have one of the most beautiful sunsets in the coast of Mexico.

The project site is situated directly facing the South Pacific Ocean, sharing 550 meters of coastline with only the breathtaking beach as the border between the water and the site. The site measures 550 meters by 490 meters, and it is sandwiched between the endless view of the South Pacific Ocean on the south side and the mountains on the north side. With such a generous length of the site, I have created a single concrete wall of 312 meters long by 3.6 meters high. It is situated 150 meters from the water cutting across the site

parallel to the coast line. The wall creates the horizontal separation between the public programs on the north side and private programs on the south side. The wall also generates the main circulation path cutting across every program serving as a dual interior and exterior wall. Rich red and orange sunset is to be reflected on the concrete surface.

The client for this project is a Mexican artist based in New York and Mexico whose red art works left me a strong impression. The project also entails having a large studio, which is situated on the south east end of the wall where he can work and create master pieces. One main large villa is situated in the center of the wall which connects the north and the south areas for his family and friends with one large open living and dining space which connects to the terrace. Six small villas for guests

are situated on the south west side of the wall. On the north east side of the wall is a large gallery space where the client can hold exhibitions open to the public.

Due to its hot weather, the roof is formed by layers of dried Royal Palm Tree leaves which are most commonly used in the region for natural air ventilation. In Mexico such roof is called Palapa. The site is very rich with wind blown from the ocean during the day and gentle breeze from the mountains through the subtle openings on the long wall during the night time; therefore, not a single glass window nor any mechanical ventilation system is used in this project except in the gallery space. Most of the interior spaces have no distinction from the exterior other than the Palapa roofs hovering over them.

The interior vertical space is formed by two essences. Above the eyelevel captures the local and traditional spirit with the Palapa roofs. Whereas below the eyelevel, captures the contemporary essence with geometric concrete walls, columns, stone floorings and the wooden shutters. Furthermore, the open space in-between unifies these two essences under one roof.

This is a very unique project with use of various uncommon materials allowing me to create architecture and spaces which cannot be created other than its location of the project. I am excited and hope to see how the artist's artwork will evolve through this project. Tadao Ando

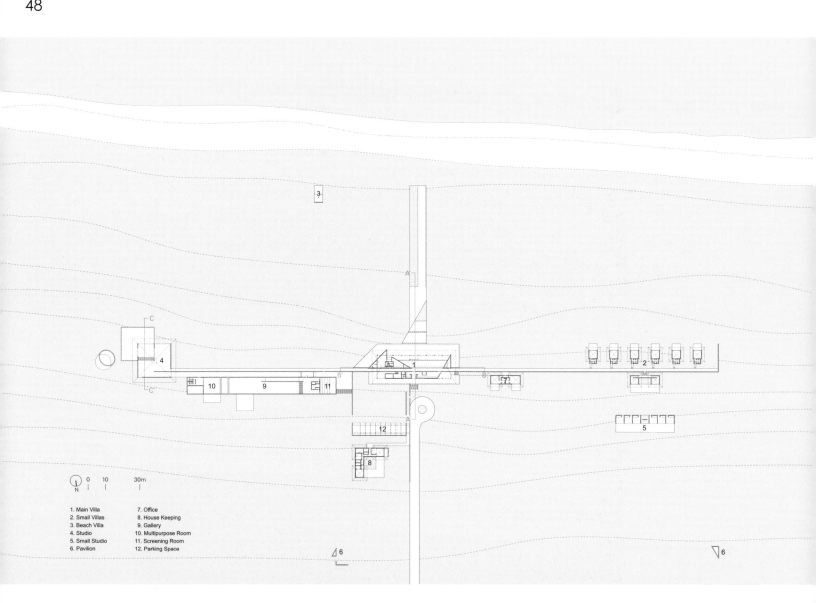

N 0 10 30m

1. Main Villa   7. Office
2. Small Villas   8. House Keeping
3. Beach Villa   9. Gallery
4. Studio   10. Multipurpose Room
5. Small Studio   11. Screening Room
6. Pavilion   12. Parking Space

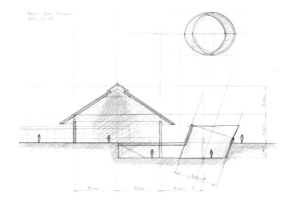

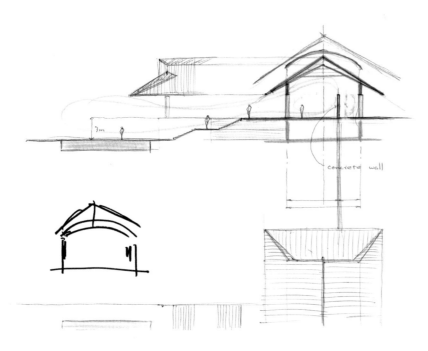

concrete wall

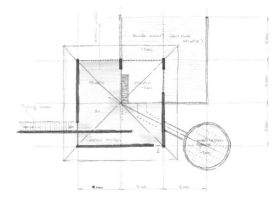

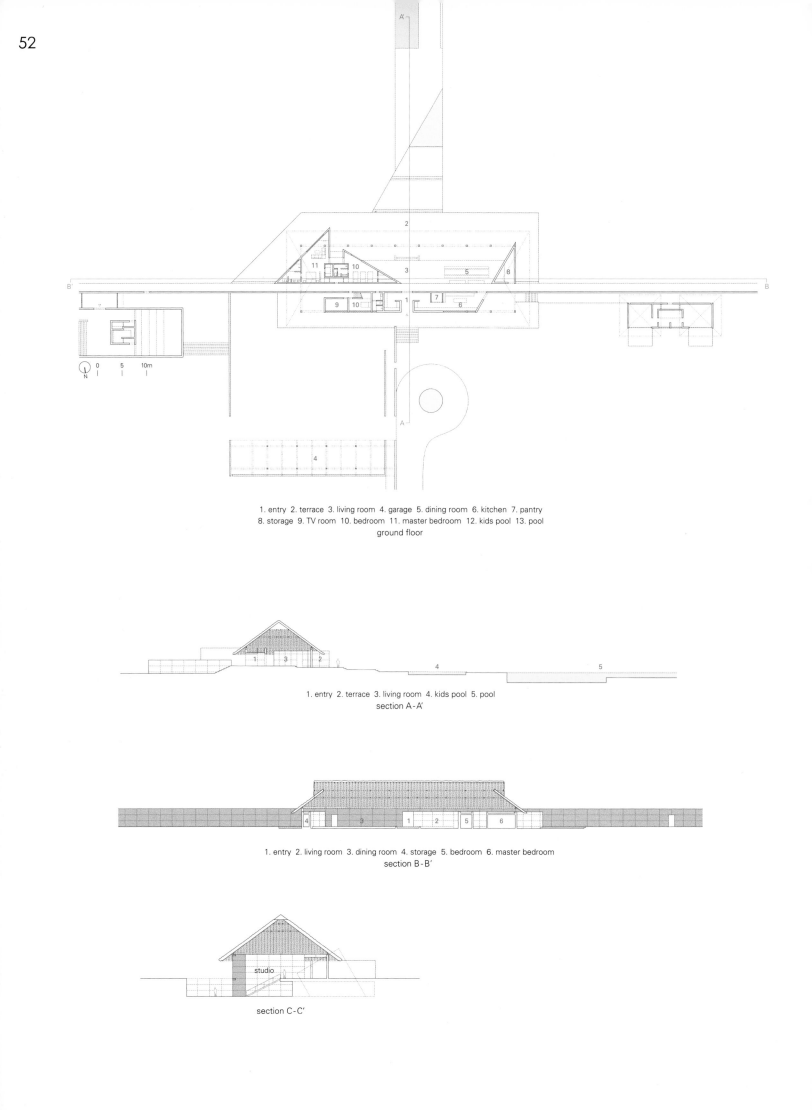

1. entry 2. terrace 3. living room 4. garage 5. dining room 6. kitchen 7. pantry
8. storage 9. TV room 10. bedroom 11. master bedroom 12. kids pool 13. pool
ground floor

1. entry 2. terrace 3. living room 4. kids pool 5. pool
section A-A'

1. entry 2. living room 3. dining room 4. storage 5. bedroom 6. master bedroom
section B-B'

studio

section C-C'

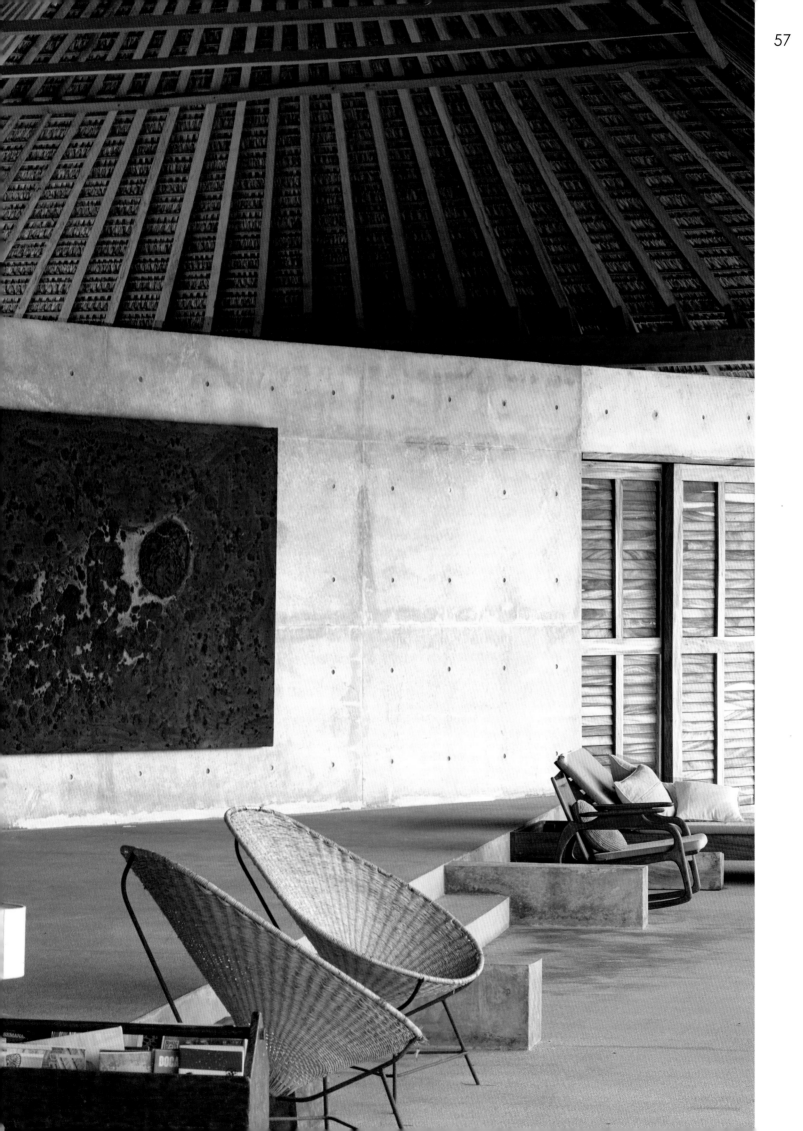

전통과 현대가 어우러진 예술가의 집

멕시코 남쪽의 항구 도시 푸에르토 에스콘디도. 숨겨진 항구라는 뜻을 가진 이름에 걸맞게 확 트인 남쪽과 달리 북쪽으로는 산맥이 끝없이 펼쳐져 있다. 남태평양을 정면으로 마주 보는 550m 길이의 해안선을 따라 고운 모래의 해변이 이어진다. 서핑하기에 좋은 파도가 넘실대 서퍼들의 성지라 불리기도 한다. 또한, 멕시코 해변 중 가장 아름다운 일몰을 감상할 수 있는 곳으로 휴양객들의 발길이 사철 끊이지 않는다.

이렇게 평화로운 해변가에 건물 설계를 의뢰한 사람은 멕시코에서 태어나 뉴욕에 기반을 두고 작품 활동을 하고 있는 예술가 보스코 소디다. 그는 이곳을 자신만의 공간이자, 가까운 예술가들을 위한 재충전의 장소, 지역의 커뮤니티를 위한 교육 시설로 만들고자 했다.

건축가는 해안선에서 150m 떨어진 곳에 길이 312m, 높이 3.6m의 콘크리트 벽을 세웠다. 동서를 가르지르는 이 벽은 북쪽의 공공 영역과, 남쪽의 개인 영역을 나눈다. 공간을 구획하는 동시에 모든 동선의 중심으로써, 외벽이 되기도 내벽이 되기도 하며 부지 내의 모든 공간에 나타난다. 또한 남태평양의 주홍빛 일몰을 그대로 받아들여 건물 안으로 끌어들인다.

콘크리트 벽의 남동쪽 끝으로는 보스코 소디가 작업하는 개인 스튜디오가 있다. 이 사적인 공간을 지나 중심부로 이동하면 넓은 빌라가 등장한다. 개방형 거실과 테라스로 연결되는 식사 공간은 남쪽에 있는 보스코의 가족과 북쪽의 친구들을 이어주는 매개공간이 된다. 남서쪽으로는 6개의 작은 손님용 빌라가 있고 북동쪽으로는 전시를 열 수 있는 커다란 갤러리 공간이 들어섰다.

지붕은 이 지역에서 사용되는 팔라파 형식을 가져왔는데 말린 대왕 야자잎을 여러 겹 겹쳐 만들었다. 긴 벽에는 개구부를 뚫어 밤낮으로 부는 산들바람이 그 사이로 넘나들도록 했다. 그래서 갤러리를 제외하고는 유리창이나 기계식 환기 시스템을 사용할 필요가 없었다.

실내공간은 이렇듯 지역 전통의 지붕과 현대성의 본질을 지닌 콘크리트 벽, 기둥, 석조 바닥, 나무 셔터 등으로 극명한 대비를 연출했다. 전통과 현대의 서로 다른 특징이 열린 공간을 통해 하나로 이어진다. 내부는 특별한 장식이나 마감을 하지 않아 외부와 큰 차이가 없다. 건물은 평범한 재료들을 다양하게 사용하여 멕시코 해변이 지닌 매력을 공간 속에서도 그대로 느낄 수 있다. 다다오 안도

Project: Bosco Studio & House / Location: Puerto Escondido, Oaxaca, Mexico
Architects: Tadao Ando Architect & Associates (Tadao Ando, Alex H. Iida)
Mexico design team: BAAQ' (Jose Alfonso Quñones, Luis Muñoz Pérez, Joaquin Castillo)_Architect of record, Javier Ribe Alfredo Athie IESSA_Structural engineer,
Jorge Ivan_Map engineer, BAAQ´CAFARO_General contractor, BAAQ/Victor Raygosa/ Juan Sodi_Concrete works, Javier Gomez; Josue Vazquez_Millwork, Alejandro Sanjines_
Roofing, Miguel Angel Dorantes_Electrical systems, Antonio Esparza_Mechanical system/Plumbing, Enedino Barragan_Doors and windows
Client: Bosco Sodi / Use: Art Studio, Gallery, Residence / Site area: 269,500m² / Bldg. area: 3,685m² / Gross floor area: 3,780m²
Structure: reinforced concrete, wood structure roof / Materials: exposed concrete_exterior wall, marmolina (granite and marble)_exterior floor, exposed concrete_interior wall,
marmolina (granite and garble)/wood flooring (parota)_interior floor, exposed concrete_ceiling, palapa_roof
Design: 2011.11~2012.12 / Construction: 2013.01~2014.10 / Photograph: ©Edmund Sumner

Project: Guan Yin Pavilion
Location: Rangsit University, Pathumthani, Thailand
Architects: Studiomake
Interior designer: Studiomake
Landscape designer: Studiomake
Structural engineer: Borvornb hun Vonganan, Adinun Teeranupatana
System engineer: Rangsit University
Contractor: Me Tha Construction & Engineering Co.,LTD.
Owner: Chinese-Thai Institute, Rangsit University
Bldg. area: 2,000m²
Construction cost: 75,000,000mb
Completion: 2015.2
Photograph: ©Spaceshift Studio (courtesy of the architect)

Guan Yin Pavilion

Studiomake

We designed the 1,500 sqm headquarter for the Chinese-Thai Institute at Rangsit University, in the center of a lake.

Rarely do we start a project from iconography or symbolism - for us, form is always a bi-product of other decisions and relationships, but this was an important gesture to our client, so we needed to shift our approach.

Our conversations always begin with material and making, and we started thinking about bricks. Thai bricks are red while Chinese bricks are grey—this has to do with the nature of the soil. For this building, which represented the academic and cultural exchange between Thailand and China, we wanted to use a grey brick. However, (of course) we weren't interested in producing the bricks in China and shipping them to Thailand.

After some researching, we found a factory who has been doing experiments in double-firing bricks. By double-firing in a special heat setting, the clay color shifts from red to grey. We immediately adopted the idea.

Our early massing studies began from this idea of a classically symmetrical building. Its entrance would be through the back in order to choreography and purposely delay the process of arrival. We set two volumes on the north and south under a single roof, and wanted them to be unified in material but differentiated in detail.

Our idea was to use a single brick in two different ways—to create a solid wall and a perforated wall. The orientation of the brick allows the peaks to be aligned in certain areas creating a crisp shadow line and offset in other areas creating a heavy texture, almost a turbulence. Tightly-spaced columns function as a screen.

The building is comprised of two masses identical in footprint and volume. To the south is a glass-enclosed exhibition hall, to the north, administrative offices, meeting rooms, a classroom, and a cafe. The open air central courtyard connects the two volumes. The entire building is covered in a single, sweeping post-tensioned concrete roof with generous overhangs. The client had always conceived of the building as a "pavilion" and wanted it to sit in a body of water, so the building is placed in the center of a natural water pond on the far side of campus. Studiomake

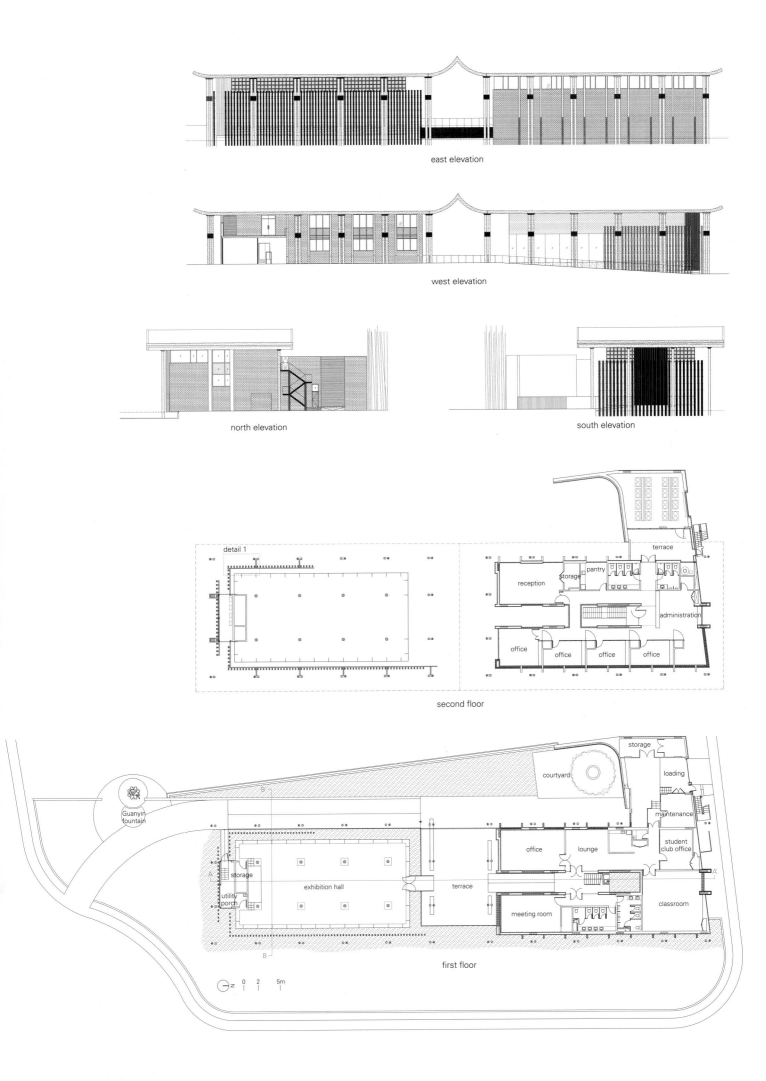

east elevation

west elevation

north elevation

south elevation

detail 1

reception

storage

pantry

terrace

administration

office

office

office

office

second floor

Guanyin
fountain

storage

loading

courtyard

maintenance

student
club office

storage

utility
porch

exhibition hall

terrace

office

lounge

classroom

meeting room

first floor

랑싯 대학교 관인 파빌리온

랑싯 대학교는 태국 방콕에 있는 사립대학교로 세계적으로 우수한 많은 대학과 활발한 국제 교류 활동을 진행하고 있다. 다양한 국적의 사람들이 모이는 대학 캠퍼스인 만큼 건물 하나를 계획하는 일에도 각기 다른 문화나 양식을 다각도로 고려해야만 한다.

태국과 중국의 학술, 문화적인 교류를 위한 '관인 파빌리온'이 캠퍼스의 북쪽 입구에 자리한 연못 한가운데 새로이 들어섰다. 건물의 정면은 연못에 둘러싸여 있어 입구는 건물의 반대편으로 돌아가야 만날 수 있다. 파빌리온은 똑같은 크기의 건물 두 개를 남쪽과 북쪽에 정확히 대칭으로 배치하고 하나의 지붕으로 덮었다. 남쪽은 유리로 덮인 전시 공간이고, 북쪽에는 행정실, 회의실, 교실, 카페가 있다. 가운데에는 탁 트인 정원이 떨어진 두 공간을 하나로 잇는다.

건축가는 이곳에 태국과 중국, 두 나라의 문화를 함께 담아내고자 했다. 각 나라의 상징이나 연상되는 이미지를 합쳐 시각화하는 일차원적인 방식에서 나아가 보다 본질적으로 접근했다. 해결의 실마리는 주재료로 벽돌을 사용하는 것이다. 태국과 중국은 토질이 다르므로 전통 벽돌의 색도 다르다. 태국은 빨갛고, 중국은 회색이다. 작업은 서로 다른 두 벽돌을 어떻게 사용할지를 고민하는 것에서 시작됐다. 수많은 연구와 조사 끝에 벽돌을 가열해 실험하는 공장을 찾아냈고, 벽돌을 두 번 구워내면 붉은색이 회색으로 변한다는 사실을 알아냈다.

또한, 벽돌은 두 가지 형태로 만들었다. 하나는 일반적인 직사각형이고, 다른 하나는 건물 지붕처럼 가운데가 뾰족하게 솟아난 모양이다. 직사각형 벽돌은 북쪽 건물에, 뾰족한 벽돌은 남쪽 건물에 사용했는데, 벽돌을 위로 길게 기둥처럼 쌓아 올려 유리로 된 남쪽 전시장을 수직으로 빙 둘러 감쌌다.

뿐만 아니라, 태국의 잦은 호우를 이겨낼 수 있도록 벽과 각 층의 바닥판은 물에 뜨는 재료를 사용했다. 스튜디오메이크

Floating Diagram

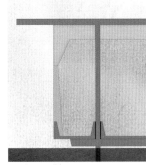

regular condition

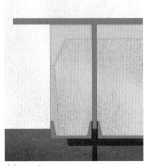

rising water

rising water and floating

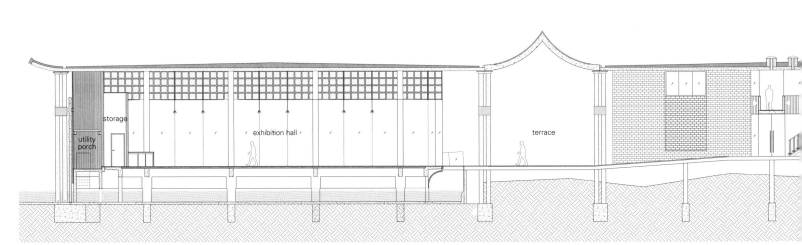

section A-A'

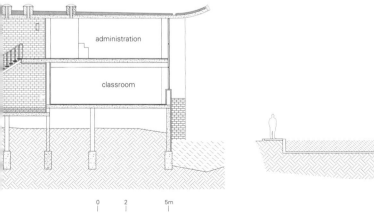

administration

classroom

0 2 5m

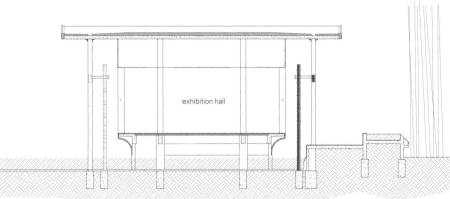

exhibition hall

section B-B'

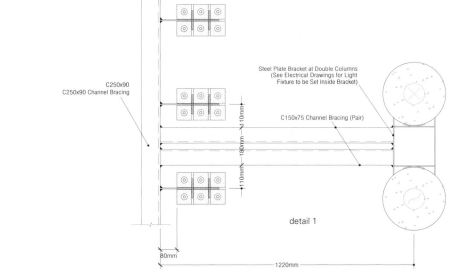

500mm 500mm

180mm

255mm

B.

400mm

C250x90
C250x90 Channel Bracing

Steel Plate Bracket at Double Columns
(See Electrical Drawings for Light
Fixture to be Set Inside Bracket)

C150x75 Channel Bracing (Pair)

110mm

180mm

110mm

detail 1

80mm

1220mm

brick prototypes after bisque firing

mock up - brick and brush

Fan Zeng Art Gallery
Original Design Studio

Fan Zeng art gallery is built for exhibition, communication, research and collection of the calligraphy, paintings and poetries, which is created by the master Fan Zeng and the Fan Family in Nantong city.

The concept of Fan Zeng art gallery started from "courtyard", an element of traditional space. In order to create an atmosphere of "making modern creations under ancient rules", the designers separate the courtyard from the physical circumstance, and then combine the visiting behavior together with thinking.

The "courtyards of relationships" is a theme of Fan Zeng art gallery. It is first reflected in the presentation of three different forms of courtyards: "well courtyard" on the ground floor, "water courtyard" and "stone courtyard" across from north to south, "encircled courtyard" on the third floor. With those courtyards, a three-dimensional courtyard framework is established, in which those courtyards play major roles. Initially, the idea of "three-dimensional courtyard" aims to decrease the volume of the building. Therefore, a big and integral volume is transferred into three smaller volumes. So, the scale of the courtyards approaches more to the scale of human body, and then can be more sensible and understandable. The

designers get themselves out of the gridding control system and make the partial relationships become a new start. The seemingly unrelated three courtyards, get assembled for their own reasons, and become unexpectedly changeable for the diverse connections between each other.

The "courtyard of visualization" is another theme. The partial relationships are juxtaposed, so that they can be presented in sequence, and therefore make it possible for people to visit and visualize. In the fragment of the scenes, relationships come to emerge one after another. Although they are juxtaposed, we can still realize the order and contact with them. They connect each other in our mind, making the seemingly mixed entirety get visualized. Art gallery advocates the "diffuse boundary" in order to break the usual separation in exhibition by a dispersed display mode. This helps build a miraculous space with widespread possible path. Its narrative mode is never formed by the central exhibition, but is leaded by the route and experience. It changes the original opposite concept of obstruction and communication in an interesting way, which gently and smoothly brings about exploratory way for visitors but still refuses to be boring or blunt. This is the beauty of so-called orient tortuousness.

N 0   20   50m

Project: Fan Zeng Art Gallery / Location: Nantong University, Nantong, Jiangsu Province / Architects: Original Design Studio / Architects in charge: Zhang Ming, Zhang Zi, Li Xuefeng, Sun Jialong, Zhang Zhiguang, Su Ting / Design company: The Architectural Design and Research Institute of Tongji University / Investor: Nantong University / Area: 7,028m² / Design: 2010.11~2013.1 / Construction: 2014.9 / Photograph: ©Yao Li (courtesy of the architect) - p.78, p.80~81, p.86~87, p.88~89bottom, p.90~91, ©Su Shengliang (courtesy of the architect) - p.85, p.89top, p.92~93

"Courtyards of artistic conception" is emphasized, too. Fan Zeng Art Gallery performs the conception of "less is more", the elaborate control of the existence, and the abounding vision and image within a gentle appearance. Instead of a strong overall framework leading the whole story with a clear rule, it produces a relatively flexible and spontaneous partial relation from the three different yards. The theme of "evolutionary relationship" means that the evolution of relationship itself plays a more important role than the evolution of every single unit. Thus the design reconstructs the relation of three yards, but does no great change in any one yard. Three yards in simple prototype are not far away from the traditional form, but they actually express extraordinary possibility after the communication and intermediation with each other. Nowadays, we usually call for modern spirit under traditional cover, so-called modern and tradition does not only rely on formality, but also requires a thinking spirit.

Fan Zeng Art Gallery is an ethereal chamber that let the water and ink blend and leaves room for halo, which makes it possible of making the light out of the strong. It represents an attitude that pays tribute to Chinese brush painting of having the universe within an inch, realizing the whole complexity with every simple part, and showing full charm with a pure spirit.

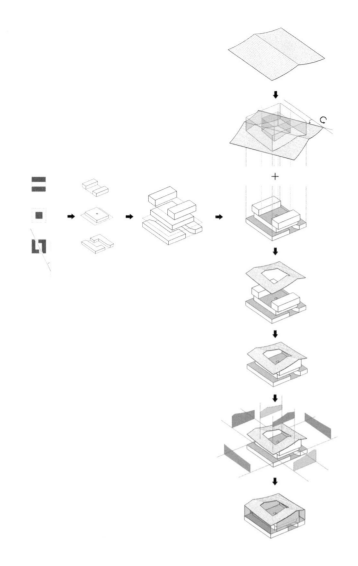

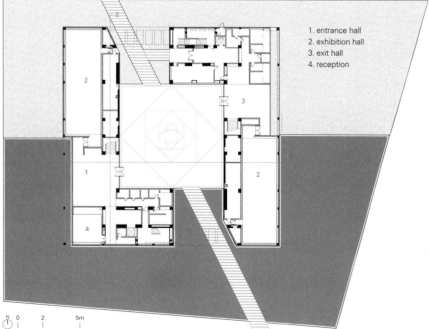

1. entrance hall
2. exibition hall
3. exit hall
4. reception

first floor

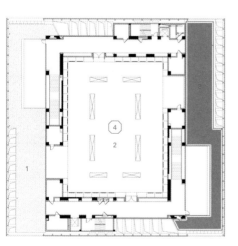

1. stone garden 2. main exibition hall
3. waterfront 4. light well (skylight)
second floor

north elevation

west elevation

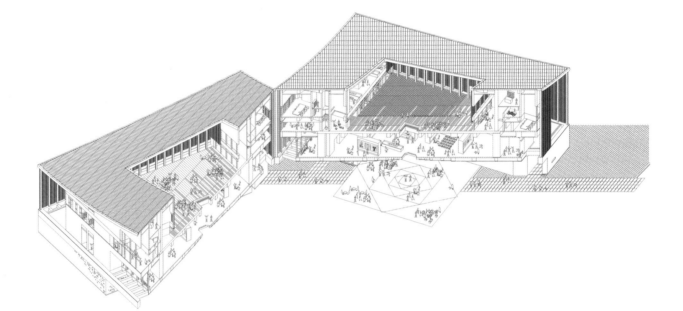

1. laboratory 2. courtyard 3. Fan Zeng studio 4. office
third floor

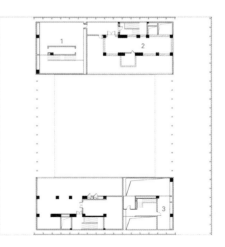

1. meeting room 2. storage 3. rest room
fourth floor

마당을 품은 미술관

미술관은 중국 장쑤성, 난퉁 시의 대가인 범증과 그 일가의 작품을 소장한다. 서예, 동양화, 한시 등의 미술품을 전시할 뿐만 아니라, 교육과 연구를 할 수 있는 공간도 마련돼 있다.

미술관 설계 개념은 동양 건축에서 중요하게 다뤄지는 공간인 '마당'에서 시작했다. 고대의 정신을 이어받아 현대의 창조물을 만들기 위해서 건축가는, 마당을 물리적 조건으로부터 완전히 분리해 새로운 방식으로 구상했다.

우선, 마당은 관계를 맺는 곳이다. 미술관은 세 개의 서로 다른 마당을 만들었다. 지상층의 우물 마당, 북측과 남측에 각각 물과 돌로 조성한 마당, 그리고 3층의 중정 마당은 내부 공간을 보다 입체적으로 만드는 중요한 역할을 한다. 세 개의 마당으로 전체 공간 또한 세 개의 작은 공간들로 나뉜다. 이는 거대한 건물을 나눠 규모를 줄이기 위해 계획 초기부터 고려된 것이다. 덕분에 마당은 휴먼 스케일에 맞춰져 섬세하게 다가온다. 나아가 건축가는 격자 공간 틀에서 벗어나 모든 공간을 전체와 부분의 관계 안에서 구상한다. 그래서 세 마당은 서로 연관되지 않은 듯 각각의 고유한 의미를 지니는 동시에, 예상치 못한 방식으로 서로 연결된다.

마당의 시각적 특성 또한 주요하게 다뤄진다. 각 공간은 나란히 놓이며 연속성을 지니기 때문에, 시각적으로도 명확하게 드러난다. 연이어 등장하는 여러 개의 단편적인 풍경들은 일정한 질서를 드러낸다. 때문

에, 혼란스러운 듯한 전체 공간안에서 부분들을 인지할 수 있다.

전시 공간은 곳곳에 흩어져 있어 미술관 내부의 경계를 흐려 놓는다. 이는 전시장을 향한 다양한 이동 경로와 동선을 가능케 하여, 공간적 경험과 여정을 제공한다. 또한, 공간을 열고 닫음에 따라 상반되는 소통 관계를 완전히 다른 관점에서 흥미롭게 접근하여, 조심스럽고 완만하지만, 지루하거나 적나라하지 않게, 새로운 공간들을 펼쳐낸다. 이렇게 구불구불하게 전개되는 공간의 아름다움은 동양 문화의 특성이기도 하다.

마지막으로, 마당은 미학적 관점에서도 강조되었다. 미술관은 전체적으로 절제된 아름다움을 드러낸다. 정교하게 설계된 공간들은 온화하면서도 풍부한 인상들로 가득하다. 명확한 계획에 따른 틀에 박힌 규정된 공간이 아니라, 각기 다른 성격의 세 마당에 의해 자연스레 생겨난 유연한 사잇 공간이다. 공간은 점점 더 밀접하게 어우러지며, 각각의 공간 보다 그사이의 관계가 더욱 중요해진다.

세 마당은 전통적인 형태와 크게 다르지 않다. 그러나 놀랍게도 서로 소통하고 영향을 미친다. 오늘날 전통은 형식만 남았다. 정신은 온데간데없고 건축은 전통이란 껍데기로 포장될 뿐이다. 그래서 오랜 시간 내려온 전통의 정신이 깃든 새로운 현대적 공간이 필요하다.

이처럼 미술관은 먹과 물이 번지고 빛과 여백이 만들어내는 관념의 공간이다. 중국의 전통 회화처럼, 붓 자국 하나에도 우주를 담아내듯이 작은 부분에도 전체를 아우르는 정신을 온전히 드러낸다.

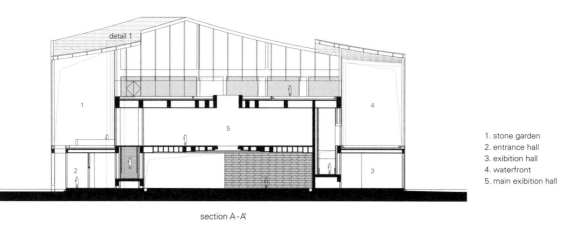

1. stone garden
2. entrance hall
3. exibition hall
4. waterfront
5. main exibition hall

section A - A'

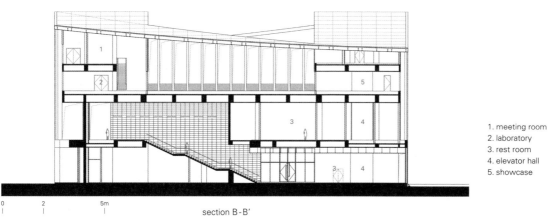

1. meeting room
2. laboratory
3. rest room
4. elevator hall
5. showcase

0   2   5m

section B - B'

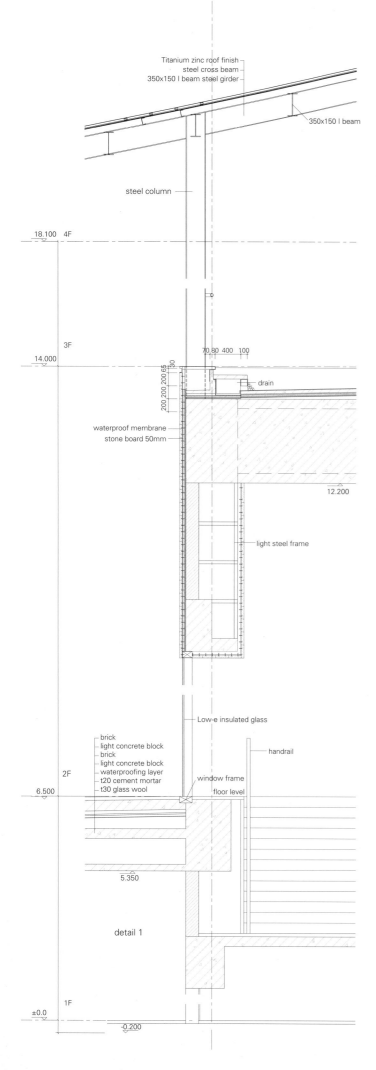

Titanium zinc roof finish
steel cross beam
350x150 I beam steel girder

350x150 I beam

steel column

18.100 4F

3F
14.000

70 80 400 100

30

200 200 200 65

drain

waterproof membrane
stone board 50mm

12.200

light steel frame

Low-e insulated glass

brick
light concrete block
brick
light concrete block
waterproofing layer
t20 cement mortar
t30 glass wool

handrail

window frame
floor level

2F
6.500

5.350

detail 1

1F
±0.0

-0.200

范曾藝術館

skylight details

ceiling structure

glass finish

stainless steel frame and
stone finish

Bridging Tradition and Innovation

Casa-Port Railway Station
AREP

The construction of the new Casa-Port railway station is part of an overall urban remodelling plan for a district located on the edge of the port of Casablanca, linking the old city to the north of the urban area. The project is also designed to keep pace with the growth in rail traffic anticipated by Moroccan Railways (ONCF).

This transport hub comprises a large passenger hall opening onto a wide square to the south-west and the platforms to the south-east, a shopping center located on the lower level of the hall, an underground car park on two levels, and an office building parallel to the platforms.

Taking into account the predominance of commuter travel and the simultaneous nature of peak traffic flows (incoming and outgoing), the passenger hall has been designed for full access to the platform concourse. Access points to the platforms are spread along the length of the hall, ensuring optimum flow management at peak times. The hall contains all the services required by travellers, including a prayer room away from bustle and noise. A wide central opening provides access to a lower level which will accommodate the shopping center, food court areas, and the underground car park.

The architecture of the station hall is characterized by its roof, a wide canopy extending beyond the façades to jut out over the square, and its supporting columns, which open out at the top to allow light to enter the building through openings in the roof. The hall's glass façades enable travellers to grasp the organization of the station and its walkways before they enter. On the west side, facing the city, a contemporary moucharaby system filters the strong afternoon sunlight without obstructing the view.

In this way, the Casa-Port station adapts to the Moroccan tradition, while reflecting the permanent modernity of the city of Casablanca.

ONCF
GARE
DE CASA-PORT
محطة
RAIL CENTER
La Pappardella
WRAPS N'GO!!

까사 항구 기차역

아프리카 최대의 항구 도시 카사블랑카. 모로코를 대표하는 관광도시이자, 많은 기업과 관공서가 밀집한 행정 도시이기도 하다. 그래서 기차역을 이용해 통근하는 이용객 수가 많아 늘 혼잡하다. 새 카사 항구 기차역은 교통량 증가로 인한 불편을 해결해 줄 도시 계획의 일부이다. 추후 지하에 들어설 고속철도와의 연결도 염두에 두고 계획됐다. 카사블랑카의 구시가지인 메디나의 교차로에 자리한 기차역은 대합실, 승강장, 쇼핑센터, 지하주차장과 사무 공간으로 이뤄진다. 남서쪽의 광장과 이어지는 커다란 대기실은 남동쪽 승강장의 중앙 홀과도 곧바로 연결된다. 효율적이고 원활한 동선을 위해 승강장으로 향하는 통로가 홀 전체를 통과하도록 배치했다.

또한, 이슬람 국가의 공공시설로서 시민들 누구나 이용할 수 있는 기도실도 대기실 한 편에 마련했다. 대기실과 승강장의 아래층에는 쇼핑센터와 지하주차장이 자리한다. 기차역 직원들의 사무 공간은 승강장과 나란히 두어 승객 지원 업무를 더 원활히 할 수 있도록 했다.

광장까지 튀어나온 거대한 캐노피 지붕이 눈에 띄는데, 이를 지지하기 위해서는 많은 기둥이 필요했다. 건물의 천장과 캐노피에는 자연광을 최대한 많이 받아들이기 위해 여러 개의 구멍을 뚫었다. 기차역 내외부에 얼기설기 서 있는 기둥들은 캐노피를 지탱하는 동시에 자연스러운 빛으로 내부 공간을 채울 수 있게 해준다.

건물 전면은 유리 위에 기하학적인 패턴 구조물을 덧대 빛과 시야를 조절한다. 이 패턴은 중세시대 이슬람 건축에서 내려온 전통 목조 격자 세공인 '마쉬라비아'에서 영감을 얻어 만들었다.

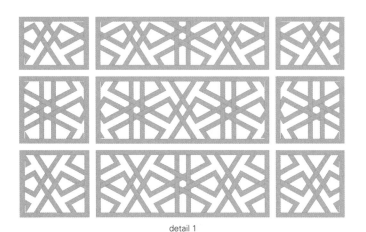

detail 1

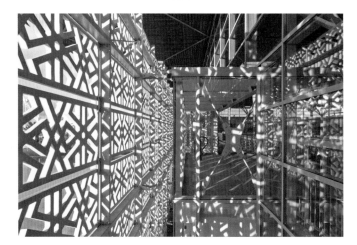

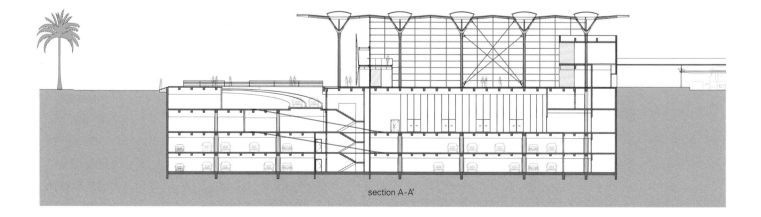

section A-A'

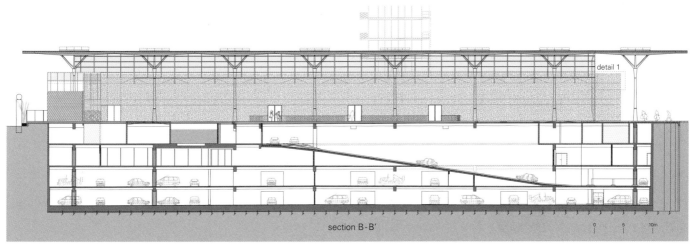

detail 1

section B - B'

0   5   10m

104

Project: Casa-Port, New railway station of Casablanca
Location: Casablanca, Morocco
Architects: AREP - Etienne Tricaud, Philippe Druesne, Christophe Iliou,
Groupe 3 Architectes - Omar Tijani, Skander Amine
Project management: AREP - Etienne Tricaud, Philippe Druesne, Christophe Iliou,
Groupe 3 Architectes - Omar Tijani, Skander Amine, Architects Vincent Missemer
Structures: MAP 3 - Emmanuel Livadiotti, Erick Cuervo
Engineering consulting firm for structuring works: UTECA, INGECOBAT
Landscape architect: Atelier Bertrand Houin
Contracting owner: ONCF
Client: Office National des Chemins de Fer marocainsm (Moroccan national rail operator)
Areas: station 2,500 sqm (including 1,000 sqm of shops), underground car park (380 spaces)
Start of work: spring 2008
Completion: 2015
Photograph: ©Didier Boy de La Tour (courtesy of the architect)

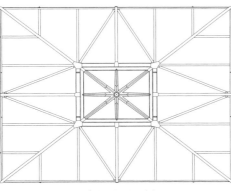

roof structure module

roof structure unit

roof structure unit cover

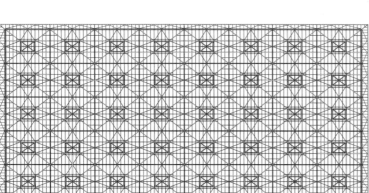

roof structure

Bridging Tradition and Innovation

Chinmaya Mission Austin
Miro Rivera Architects

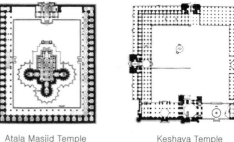

Atala Masjid Temple
Jaunpur, India

Keshava Temple
Mysuru, India

Established as a home for the Central Taxas division of Chinmaya Mission, an international non-profit Hindu spiritual organization, this new 8-acre campus is characterized by an architectural language that reinterprets traditional Indian typologies in order to reflect the organization's modern context. Presented with the unique opportunity of designing a Hindu mission in Central Texas, the architects applied their knowledge of local building materials to create a visual language that is rich in texture, sculptural in quality, and innovative in design.

The main challenge of the project was two-fold: to creates that accommodated both the spiritual and practical needs of the rapidly-growing mission, and to apply established Hindu practices in ways that felt new and unexpected. The campus master plan combines the traditional vastu shastra principles

of Hindu design-emphasizing geometric patterns, symmetry, and directional alignments-with a contemporary sensibility. The completed first phase consists of a temple and Bala Vihar(educational building) arranged around a central lawn, with space reserved for future buildings.

Working within the restrictive budget of a non-profit organization, design was not sacrificed; rather, it inspired the design team to find a vocabulary that was simple yet refined. In elevation, white stucco walls and pitched roofs recall traditional Indian typologies; large windows provide abundant natural light in every occupied space; and deep overhangs offer refuge from the hot Texas sun. By simply alternating the tones of the standing seam metal roof panels, a striking design motif was conjured up from a commonplace material. The most spectacular example of this creative adaptability is the airy

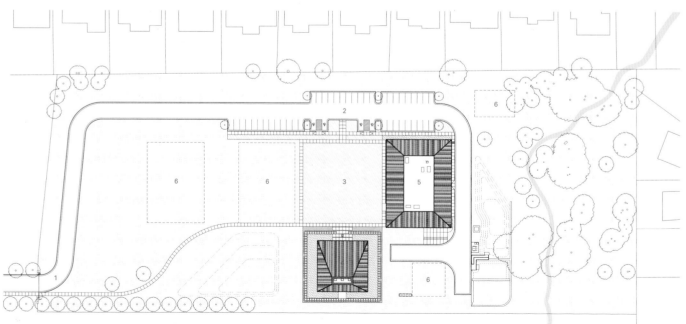

1. entry/gate 2. parking 3. courtyard 4. temple 5. Bala Vihar 6. future building

steeple atop the temple's peak. To galvanized fencing material and then lifted into place.

Serving as the educational hub of the mission center, the Bala Vihar consists of 12 classrooms plus a central gallery and large covered patio for congregation and social events. Flexibility was a major priority, as the facility must comfortably accommodate small weekly classes as well as special events. In response, three of the classrooms utilize operable partitions to create larger spaces as needed. A central gallery plays multiple roles as circulation, display space, and assembly hall.

At the temple, the prevalence of symmetry and geometry are reminders of traditional Hindu religious architecture. Beginning in the central meditation hall and moving out toward the perimeter of locally-source limestone blocks, a series of concentric circles, squares, and rectangles-including an il-

luminated pattern in the meditation hall's dramatically-sloped ceiling-references traditional mandala-inspired architecture. Above the shrine, the most sacred space in the temple, light from concealed skylight is reflected by a golden wall, creating an aura around three deities arrayed with bright robes and flowers.

In its development and execution, the design of Chinmaya Mission Austin strikes a delicate balance between the need to respect both the traditional building methods of an ancient religion and the limited resources of a non-profit organization; and the desire to employ a contemporary aesthetic that reflects the forward-thinking approach of an international faith.

east elevation _ Bala Vihar

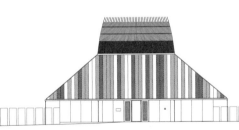

north elevation _ temple

west elevation _ Bala Vihar

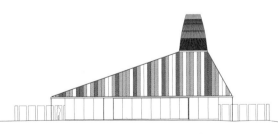

west elevation _ temple

0   5   10m

친마야 힌두교 사원

미국 텍사스주 오스틴, 한적한 동네에 힌두교 사원이 들어섰다. 국제 비영리 힌두교 단체인 친마야 미션 재단은 32,000m²에 이르는 드넓은 부지 안에 인도 전통 건축을 오늘날의 건축 언어로 재해석한 새로운 공간을 만들었다.

작업은 두 가지를 염두에 두고 시작했다. 하나는 지역에서 빠르게 성장한 힌두 사원이 제 기능을 할 만큼 충분한 공간을 확보하는 것이고, 또 하나는 힌두교 사상을 신도들과 주변 지역 주민들까지도 색다른 방식으로 경험할 수 있게 하는 것이다.

먼저, 형태와 공간 배치에 '바스투 사스트라'라는 인도의 전통 건축의 원리를 적용했다. 기하학적 형태와 대칭성 등 많은 사원이 갖는 보편적 공간 구성을 기본으로 삼았다. 여기에 지역 고유의 자재에 대한 이해와 지식을 바탕으로 풍부한 질감과 독특한 조형을 더했다.

예배당과 교육관은 잔디로 만든 뜰을 가운데 두고 기역 자로 놓았고, 한쪽은 향후 증축을 대비해 비워뒀다.

장방형의 예배당은 대칭을 이루는 기하학적 형태로 힌두교 전통 건축을 닮았다. 건물 주위로는 지역에서 난 석회석으로 직사각형 담장을 나란히 세워, 예배당 주위를 거닐 수 있는 회랑이 되었다.

외관의 하얀 치장 벽돌과 경사지붕은 전통 인도 건축 양식을 떠올리게 한다. 커다란 창 사이로는 충분한 빛을 끌어들이는 한편, 텍사스의 강렬한 태양을 피하기 위해 처마를 길게 뺐다. 지붕은 색색의 금속 판재로 덮었다. 이처럼 평범한 재료를 이용한 참신한 독창성은 지붕 위로 우뚝 솟은 첨탑에서도 잘 드러난다. 빛의 통로 역할을 하는 이 탑은, 울타리에 흔히 쓰이는 아연 도금의 철재로 만들어졌다.

내부로 들어서면 중앙의 명상 공간과 마주한다. 극도로 기울어진 천장에는 전통 문양인 만다라를 새긴 조명으로 신성한 분위기를 더했다. 철제 탑 안으로 떨어지는 빛이 제단 위 금빛 벽에 반사되어, 화려하게 치장한 세 신상을 은은하게 비춘다.

또 다른 건물인 교육관은 12개의 교실과 전시실, 그리고 사교 모임을 위한 안마당으로 구성된다. 이 건물에서는 유연한 공간이 핵심이다. 매주 소규모로 열리는 수업이나 특별한 행사가 열릴 때마다 자유롭게 공간을 사용하도록 하기 위해서다. 이를 위해 세 개의 교실은 필요에 따라 여닫을 수 있는 칸막이를 두었다. 상황에 따라 변하는 공간 중심에는 전시실이 들어서 다목적으로 사용할 수 있다.

Project: Chinmaya Mission Austin
Location: 12825 Burnet Road, Austin, TX, 78727
Architects: Miró Rivera Architects
Design partners: Juan Miro (FAIA LEED AP),
Miguel Rivera (FAIA LEED AP)
Project architect/manager: Ken Jones (AIA LEED AP)
Design team: Bud Franck, Spencer Cook, Matthew Helveston,
Michael Hsu, Shane Pavonetti, Edward Richardson
Civil engineer: Aupperle Company
Structural engineer: Architectural Engineers Collaborative (AEC)
MEP engineer: Bay & Associates
Lighting: ArcLight Design
Accessibility: The Access Partnership
Landscape: Studio DWG
Specialty metal work: Metalink Corporation
General contractor: SpawGlass
Client: Chinmaya Mission Austin
Site area: 8.1acres (351,354sf)
Bldg. area: temple_4,185sf, Bala Vihar_10,460sf,
conditioned_8,515sf, non-conditioned_1,945sf
Design: 2011~2013
Completion: 2014
Photograph: ©Paul Finkel (courtesy of the architect)

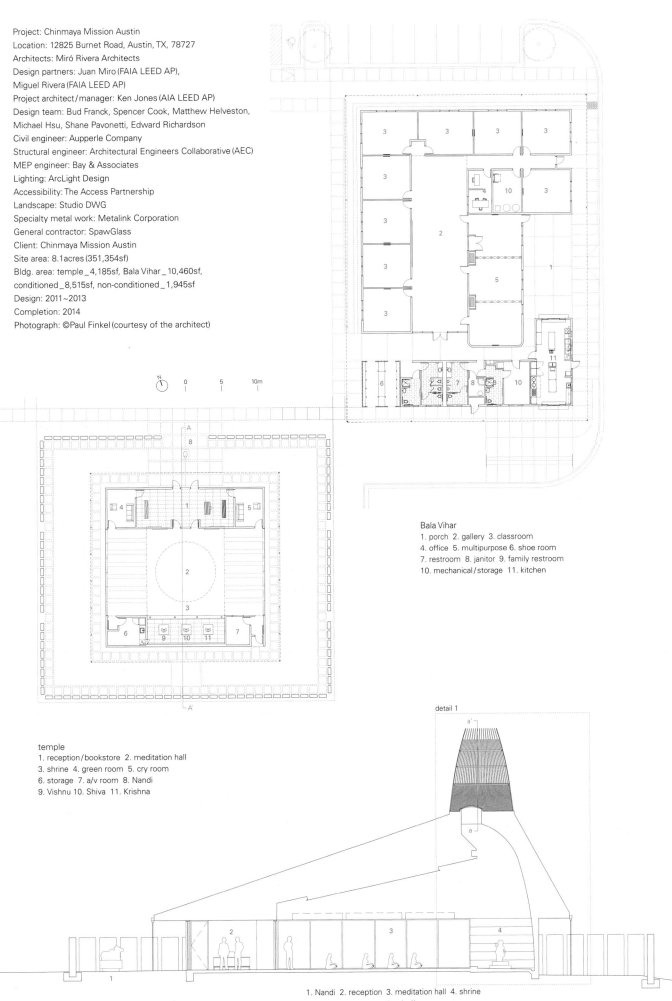

Bala Vihar
1. porch 2. gallery 3. classroom
4. office 5. multipurpose 6. shoe room
7. restroom 8. janitor 9. family restroom
10. mechanical/storage 11. kitchen

temple
1. reception/bookstore 2. meditation hall
3. shrine 4. green room 5. cry room
6. storage 7. a/v room 8. Nandi
9. Vishnu 10. Shiva 11. Krishna

detail 1

1. Nandi 2. reception 3. meditation hall 4. shrine
section A - A'

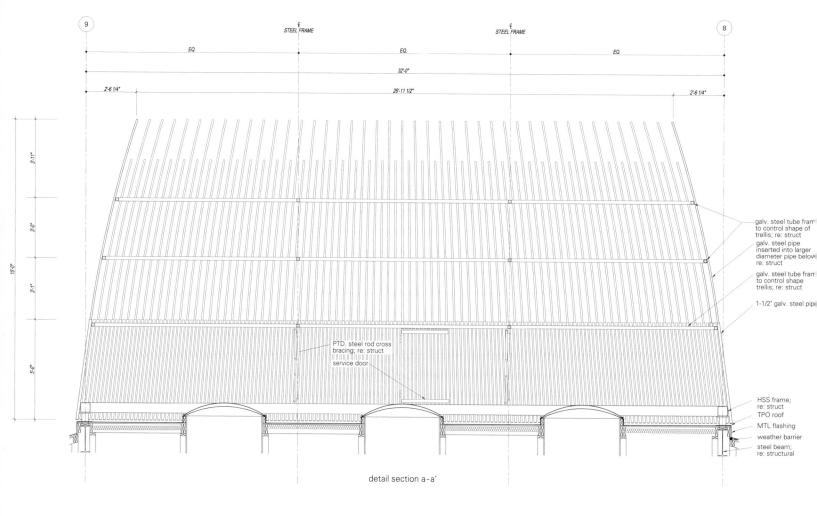

galv. steel tube fram
to control shape of
trellis; re: struct

galv. steel pipe
inserted into larger
diameter pipe below
re: struct

galv. steel tube fram
to control shape
trellis; re: struct

1-1/2" galv. steel pip

PTD. steel rod cross
bracing; re: struct

service door

HSS frame;
re: struct

TPO roof

MTL flashing

weather barrier

steel beam;
re: structural

detail section a-a'

EQ.   EQ.   EQ.

32'-0"

2'-6 1/4"   26'-11 1/2"   2'-6 1/4"

STEEL FRAME   STEEL FRAME

9   8

3'-11"

3'-0"

3'-1"

5'-0"

15'-0"

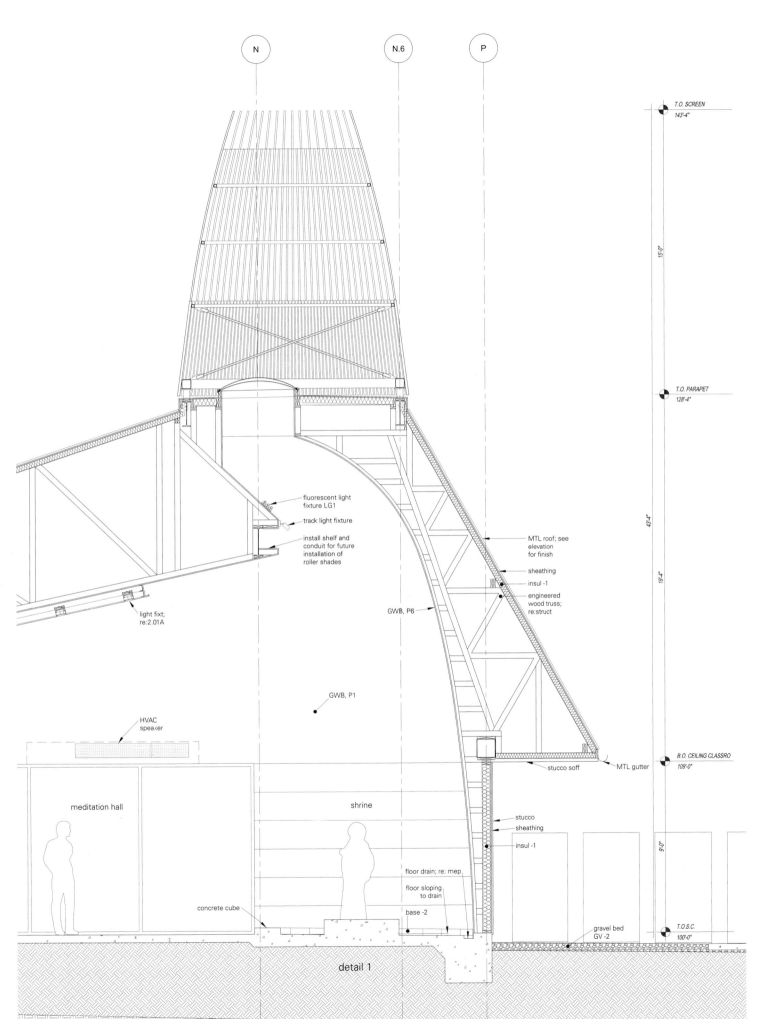

N   N.6   P

T.O. SCREEN
143'-4"

15'-0"

T.O. PARAPET
128'-4"

43'-4"

fluorescent light
fixture LG1

track light fixture

install shelf and
conduit for future
installation of
roller shades

MTL roof; see
elevation
for finish

sheathing

insul -1

19'-4"

engineered
wood truss;
re:struct

light fixt;
re:2.01A

GWB, P6

GWB, P1

HVAC
speaker

B.O. CEILING CLASSRO
109'-0"

stucco soff

MTL gutter

meditation hall

shrine

stucco

sheathing

insul -1

9'-0"

floor drain; re: mep

floor sloping
to drain

base -2

concrete cube

gravel bed
GV -2

T.O.S.C.
100'-0"

detail 1

New Indian Identities and Architectural Tectonics

New Indian Id and Architect

What is India's contemporary architectural identity, and where do its roots lie? With India's diverse cultural landscape, its colonial heritage, its various climates and geographies, is there an archetypical identity for its architectural lexicon? If so, how does it manifest itself? From the history of craft development, through the cultural transformations wrought by trade and encounters with colonial powers and the metamorphosis into a young democracy, what are the influences that have been integrated into India's visual culture and architectural language? After independence, there was a florescence of nationalism. To question and to define Indian singularity, Mahatma Gandhi looked to the traditionalist past, while the first prime minster of India, Jawaharlal Nehru, rejected British legacies and its colonial vernacular, looking forward to the future through an endorsement of modernism.

In 1950, Nehru invited Le Corbusier to design and construct the new city of Chandigarh.

오늘날 인도 건축은 정체성 탐색기에 서 있다. 많은 이들이 인도 건축의 정체성을 확립하기 위해 활발한 논의를 펼치고 있지만, 이를 한 단어로 정의하기는 어렵다. 길고 복잡한 역사를 거치며 다양한 문화적 풍경이 혼재됐고, 국토의 거대한 면적만큼이나 기후와 지형도 각양각색이기 때문이다. 이러한 인도의 문화는 다른 국가와의 관계 속에서 형성됐다 해도 과언이 아니다. 근대 이전에는 오랫동안 세계 무역의 중심지로서 다양한 문화를 접했고, 식민시대를 거치며 서구의 영향을 받기도 했으며, 민주주의 체제가 정착된 후로는 더욱 다양하고 새로운 사상에 눈을 띄게 된 것이다.

여기서 잠시 지난 한 세기 동안 인도가 겪었던 변화를 살펴보자. 19세기 후반, 영국의 식민지가 된 인도는 강한 민족적 결속력을 바탕으로 1947년 독립하게 된다. 당시 인도인들의 정신적 지주였던 마하트마 간디는 과거의 전통에서 자신들의 정체성을 찾으며 민족주의 운동을 펼쳤고, 그 영향을 받아 독립 직후의 인도는 강한 국가주의적 성향을 띠었다. 그러나 초대 총리였던 자와할랄 네루는 식민시대의 유산은 거부하면서도 서구에서 발전한 모

New Indian Identities and Architectural Tectonics / Gihan Karunaratne

entities
ural Tectonics

인도성과 인도 건축

Le Corbusier's scheme abjured India's colonial past and inspired the country's future architectural vocabulary. Government institutions and other important building clients soon adopted this version of modernism – the International style – eschewing traditional social and cultural typologies. With the advent of economic liberalization in the latter years of the twentieth century, India was exposed to new ideas and was able to access new materials and services from rest of the world. India's architecture again exhibited many western architectural attributes and renounced cultural idioms.[1] Today, however, architects and designers are looking to the past and celebrating and drawing on India's cultural heritage to explore new identities and architectural tectonics. The article explores numerous current architectural examples, from private residences and religious community buildings to an Architect's own office, to investigate and understand India's architectural pedigree and address the question of its contemporary architectural identity.

더니즘을 통해 인도의 미래를 그려내고자 했다. 대표적인 예가 1950년 시작된 찬디가르 도시계획이다. 르 코르 뷔지에는 모더니즘 건축을 적극 도입함으로써 진보적 가치를 담아낸 20세기형 신도시를 제안했는데, 그 과정에 서 전통은 완전히 배제되었다. 자유경제 체제가 도입된 20세기 후반, 인도는 또 한 번 다른 국면을 맞이하게 된 다. 새로운 사상들을 접하게 되면서 건축 역시 서구권의 특성을 띠게 된 것이다. 그러나 전통에 대한 관심은 여 전히 미약하기만 했다.

최근 들어서야 건축가들은 과거를 되돌아보기 시작했다. 보다 적극적으로 전통의 가치를 찾고, 이를 인도 건축 의 정체성을 이루는 중요한 요소로 바라보며, 이러한 특성을 반영해 새로운 공간들을 제시하는 것이다. 이 장에 서는 저마다의 특색을 지닌 주택에서부터 종교적 성향을 띤 공동체 시설까지, 인도 건축의 현주소를 보여주는 다양한 작업을 소개한다. 이 작품들을 통해 인도 건축의 계보를 되짚어보면서 이 시대 인도 건축의 정체성은 무 엇일지를 함께 고민해보자.

Säynätsalo Town Hall, Finland, 1951, Alvar Aalto

New Indian Identities and Architectural Tectonics

Globalization and critical regionalism have had, and are having, an important impact on India's architecture. We live in a globalised world, with an ever more immediate access to ideas, economies, cultures, traditions and international practices. In the 1960s and '70s most of the construction in the sub-continent exemplified modernism or the International Style; the architecture that came out of that time was somewhat generic and similar. This type of architecture had did not prioritise the relationships with local cultures, materials and geographical contexts. In general, it ignored the issue of context, including historical precedents.[2]

The term "regionalism" was first adopted by Alexander Tzonis and Liane Lefaivre, and subsequently by Prof. Kenneth Frampton in Towards a critical Regionalism: Six points of Architecture of Resistance. Frampton developed the concept of "critical regionalism", the creation of regional schools that are influenced by global architecture and ideas but which adapt them to specific contexts and so imbue architectural practice with a "sense of place" and some peculiar identity.[3]

In his essay "Critical to adopt" Frampton argues that modernism should embrace regional architectural expression. He does not, however, advocate the adoption of or reference to customs and traditions, or to local forms of architecture from the past. Rather, he argues for the recognition of current conditions of life – ways of living, culture, geography and climate – in order to form the "local tectonic form". This, Frampton writes, should serve as the regional covenant of an architectural practice.[4]

In the Western context, according to Frampton, Alvar Aalto's Säynätsalo Town Hall is one of the finest examples of critical regionalist architecture. Rational and functional, it exhibits its cultural pedigree through the use of materials such as brick

인도성과 인도 건축

국가의 경계가 무색해진 21세기, 다양성은 이 시대를 관통하는 가장 중요한 가치로 떠오르고 있다. 오늘날 우리는 언제 어디서든 다양한 사상과 가치관, 문화를 접할 수 있으며 심지어 다른 경제권의 시장에 진입하는 것마저도 그리 어려운 일은 아니다.

그러나 세계화와 지역주의라는 개념은 여전히 인도 건축에 큰 영향을 미치는듯하다. 1960~70년대만 해도 인도 건축의 경향은 지금과 사뭇 달랐다. 문화와 재료, 지형과 기후, 나아가 전통에 이르기까지 사실상 모든 측면에서 지역적인 맥락을 배제하고 전 세계적 보편성을 추구하려는 국제주의적 흐름을 따랐기 때문이다.

'지역주의'는 건축이론가 알렉산더 초이스와 리안 르페브르에 의해 제시된 용어인데, 1980년대 케네스 프램프톤의 '중대한 지역주의'로 발전하며 현대건축의 중요한 이론으로 자리 잡게 되었다. 보편적 원리를 수용하되 '장소성'에도 주목하여, 모더니즘의 획일성을 탈피하고 그 건축물만의 정체성을 불어넣어야 한다는 개념이다. 또한, 한발 더 나아가 건축은 지역성도 담아내야 한다고 주장했는데, 여기서의 지역성이란 단순히 전통건축의 요소를 모방하는 것이 아니며 현재라는 배경 속에서 재해석되어야 함을 강조했다.

이러한 관점에서 프램프톤은 서구권에서 지역주의를 대변하는 대표적인 사례로 핀란드 건축가 알바 알토의 '새이내트살로 시청사'를 꼽는다. 합리성과 기능성이라는 현대건축의 보편적 가치를 담아내면서도 벽돌과 목재 등을 이용해 지역적 특성을 적극적으로 드러내고 있다는 것이다.

Gandhi Smarak Sangrahalaya, Ahmedabad, India, 1963, Charles Correa

and timber – in particular, birch – which serve to integrate the building with the dense landscape.

Sri Lankan architect Geoffrey Bawa practised the true principles and philosophies of critical regionalism. His architecture is grounded in the historical context and architectural heritage of Sri Lanka, yet is also an accomplished and intelligent amalgamation of that pedigree with contemporary living.

In India, and in keeping with Frampton's critical regionalist philosophies, Charles Correa's Gandhi Smarak Sangrahalaya in Ahmedabad is a fine example of the principles of regionalism. The building is Correa's conscious attempt to hybridize modernity with regionalism by adopting a network of interconnecting open-to-sky spaces to restore the Gandhian philosophy of self-sufficient village community.[5]

Correa studied the fundamentals of the site in depth and developed the concept of the project in response to the site conditions. He used courtyard louvres, pergolas, local building materials and bodies of water to realize a climatically responsive design. Furthermore, Correa used vernacular materials such as brick, stone for the floor, and tile for the roof, and married them with concrete, steel and other industrial products to give the building an architectural identity.[6]

Inheriting a rich history of architecture, with influences ranging from the Moors to British colonialists to the International Style, India's architects are redefining the nation's current identity.

The following projects explore the different ways in which architects in India are adopting some of Frampton's 'critical regionalism' while acknowledging contemporary cultural realities and modern lifestyles, and by so doing are giving a new direction to Indian vernacular.

The architecture of Architecture Brio, S+PS Architects, Archohm Consults, SPASM Design Architects and Studio Sa-

스리랑카의 열대 모더니즘을 완성했다는 평을 받고 있는 건축가 제프리 바와. 그의 작업들은 자국의 역사와 문화 속에 현대적 가치들을 녹여 냄으로써 지역주의가 진정으로 지향하는 바가 무엇인지를 보여주고 있다.

찰스 꼬레아의 대표작인 '간디 추모 기념관'도 지역주의의 원리가 잘 드러난 건축물이다. 이 건물에서는 지역주의와 모더니즘이라는 상반된 가치를 의도적으로 뒤섞는다. 기념관은 여러 동의 건물로 구성되는데, 하늘을 향해 열린 중정이 모든 건물을 하나로 아우르면서 간디가 제시했던 자급 자족적 마을 공동체의 개념을 공간적으로 구현하고 있다. 이뿐만 아니라 건물에 적용된 요소들에서도 지역성에 대한 깊은 고민이 묻어난다. 안뜰, 정자를 비롯한 각종 정원 구조물과 미늘 창문을 활용해 열대 기후에 대응하며, 벽돌과 타일 등의 전통적 재료

와 콘크리트, 철재 등의 현대적 재료를 조화시켜 독특한 특성을 만들어 낸 것이다.

오래전부터 이어져 온 무어인들의 문화, 식민시대에 흡수된 영국적 양식, 근대화 시기에 지향했던 국제주의까지, 인도 건축은 복잡했던 역사만큼이나 풍성한 이야깃거리를 가지고 있다. 그리고 지금은 이를 자양분 삼아 자신들만의 건축적 정체성을 정립해가는 중이다. 이 장에서는 총 다섯 개의 인도 건축물을 소개한다. 프램프톤의 중대한 지역주의를 현대적 배경 속에 녹여내려는 이 시도들을 통해 오늘날 인도 건축이 어떤 방향으로 나아가고 있는지를 함께 살펴보자.

처음으로 소개할 언덕바지 작은 집은 인근에서 구할 수 있는 재료를 이용해 모더니즘을 토속적으로 재해석한 사례다. 이 집은 근처에 강이

Riparian House, Architecture Brio

©Ariel Huber

meep Pedora and Associates acknowledges regional culture. Sensitivity to site, context, climate and heritage is married to functionality and to the choice of appropriate materials.

In the Riparian House by Architecture Brio, the architect has used locally produced materials which remain integral to the sense of vernacular modernism. The dwelling is settled into the landscape, which camouflages and conceals the design. There is no attempt to keep nature out, or to control it. Instead, the intention has been to design and construct a building that dissolves into the landscape. The design brings together nature and architectural space in harmony. Here is an architecture that exists in sympathy with its site. This architecture celebrates the relationship of inside and out by adopting a courtyard, projected eaves, and exposed structures amplified by vistas.[7]

Such architectural language is concerned with architectural principles, a sense of intimacy and the establishment of a fluid

kinship between inside and outside. The Riparian House is a dwelling that references its natural landscape while accommodating a present day lifestyle.

The house's inhabitants move through spaces, some of which are open to the elements, that express the vibrant sprit of the locality and context. The architect has assumed the role of a craftsman by using local materials to create a modern and a regionalist building.

The architecture of the Collage House by S+PS Architects is also in a regionalist style that combines the vernacular with modernism to produce an architectural identity with a decorative aesthetic typical of south Asia. Its reconciliation of a regionalist approach with traditional typologies gives it a markedly hybridized cultural quality. Spatial attributes are complemented by the selection of materials: walls constructed from the excavated site; vertically stacked glass drum; and a composed brick arrangement. There is a continuous spatial

흐르는 전원적인 풍경 한가운데 자리하고 있다. 이러한 주변 맥락을 따르기 위해 건물은 자연을 지배하기보다는 자연에 지배당하는 쪽을 택하며 모든 공간을 풍경 속에 숨겨 버린다. 존재감을 드러내기보다는 대지에 흡수되지만, 아이러니하게도 바로 그 덕분에 이 집은 여기에 존재할 수 있었던 것이다. 여러 개의 안뜰, 돌출된 처마, 주변을 향해 열린 개구부 등, 다양한 장치들은 정교하게 조합되어 내밀하면서도 유연하게 흐르는 공간을 만들어 낸다. 안과 밖의 경계는 흐려지고 건물과 대지는 더욱 깊은 관계를 형성한다. 집 안을 거닐다 보면 때로는 있는 그대로의 자연을 맞닥뜨리기도 한다. 이렇듯 거주자들은 집 안에서도 대지의 고유한 맥락을 생생하게 경험할 수 있다. 이뿐만 아니라 자연을 그대로 받아들이면서도 오늘날의 생활 방식에 적합한 현대적인 공간을 갖추고 있는 점 역시 이 사례에서 주목할 만한 부분이다.

다음 사례인 콜라주 주택은 이름 그대로 다양한 요소를 조각보처럼 짜깁기해 흥미로운 결과물을 만들어 낸다. 여기서는 인도 건축 특유의 장식미를 지역성의 요소로 활용한다. 이러한 접근방식은 전통과 현대는 물론 다양한 문화를 아우르며 복합적 색채의 공간을 형성한다. 이 집에서 특히 주목할 점은 '재활용'으로, 주변에서 구한 갖가지 자재와 가구, 장식물 등이 다양하게 사용됐다는 것이다. 땅을 팔 때 나온 돌로 외벽을 쌓는가 하면, 유리를 겹겹이 세워 반원형으로 굽어진 내벽을 만들기도 한다. 그 밖에도 내부공간에서는 옛것과 새것, 거침과 매끄러움이 끊임없이 교차되면서 매 순간 다른 장면이 연출된다. 이러한 조화의 매력이 정점을 이룬 공간은 건물 중심부에 조성된 안뜰이다. 다양한 요소에 빛과 그림자까지 뒤섞이며 어디에서도 볼 수 없는 독특한 매력을 발산한다.

Collage House, S+PS Architects

©Sebastian Zachariah

fluidity, and a toying with old and new, smooth and rough. The typology is further refined in the central courtyard which serves the house as an extension of the inside, and in the architect's command of light and shade.

Collage House offers a contemporary domestic architectural design solution for urban living with reference to South Asian traditions, an appreciation of the architectural frame of reference, and a sympathetic palette of materials. The use of salvaged elements, which contrast with the materials of contemporary architecture, demonstrate an avant-garde embodiment of localism. By reclaiming architectural elements does the architect generate a new architectural typology?[8]

The deployment of reclaimed materials or artifacts serves to announce a sense of place in a sanitized architectural landscape. When set against the postmodern habit of adopting and echoing attributes from one's architectural heritage, the architect has instead integrated a direct historical reference or collage in the architecture and has celebrated it by making it a focal point of the building, adding an element of "bricolage".[9]

Through the use of salvaged architectural elements, colors and textures are heightened within interior spaces. At another level, the architect is exploring territory such as history and context, restoration and reconstruction, memory and decay. By contrast, the National Institute for Faith Leadership by Archohm Consults is, as the architect mentions, "devoid of design as decoration." The spaces "evoke bare thought," and "bold architectural impressions [are] intended to push people towards brave expressions." On this project, the Architect writes, "the play of light in space and in time both brought in the required ethic and aesthetic to the institution." There are architectural references from modernist hybrid vernacular forms and borrowings from Louis Kahn's vocabulary, for example, a large reinforced circular opening familiar from the Phillips Exeter Academy Library and the National Assembly

이렇듯 이 집은 인도의 전통에 기반해 새로운 형태의 도시 주거를 제안한다. 지역성은 현대적 재료와 대조를 이루는 재활용 자재를 통해 극대화되며, 평범한 풍경 속에 새로운 장소성을 부여한다. 많은 건축가들이 역사적 가치를 인정받은 건축물에서만 전통을 찾으려 하는 것과는 달리, 재료에 묻어 있는 시간의 흔적 그 자체를 전통으로 치환시키는 것이다. 이러한 과정을 통해 다시금 생명력을 갖게 된 건축 요소들은 내부 공간을 더욱 풍요롭게 만든다. 어쩌면 건축가는 이 작업을 통해 역사와 맥락, 재생과 복원, 그리고 기억이라는 영역을 탐구하는 중이었을지도 모른다.

그런가 하면 이슬람 리더쉽 교육 센터에서는 전작과는 반대로 장식이 사라진다. 그대신 공간의 민낯을 그대로 드러내 순수한 관념을 이끌어 내고, 빛으로 아름다운 시각적 효과를 연출함으로써 종교적 가치를 표

현한다. 건물의 모든 공간들은 이슬람교의 교리에 따라 외부를 향해서 닫혀있으며, 천창들을 통해서만 빛을 들인다.

건축 원리는 전통건축과 근대건축, 양쪽 모두를 참고한 듯하다. 루이스 칸의 필립스 액시터 아카데미 도서관과 방글라데시 국회의사당에서와같이 이 건물에서도 거대한 원형 개구부가 중요한 건축 요소로 쓰이고 있다. 이러한 개구부를 통해 내부로 끌어들인 빛은 공간에 상징성을 더하는 요소로 활용된다. 또한, 돌출된 처마에는 별 모양의 구멍이 다양한 크기로 뚫려있는데 이 구멍으로 떨어지는 빛과 그림자는 시시각각 다른 모습으로 바뀌며 역동적인 분위기를 조성한다. 이 건물에서는 실외 복도와 테라스 등의 공간도 중요한 역할을 하고 있다. 때로는 안뜰을 향해, 때로는 그 너머를 향해 펼쳐진 각기 다른 풍경들을 선사하며 단순한 사이 공간을 넘어선 소통의 장이 되는 것이다.

National Institute for Faith Leadership, Archohm Consults

Building of Bangladesh. Such architectural features encourage natural light to penetrate deep into the interior space. Light is not only celebrated in its physical qualities, but is also revered for its symbolic and inspirational dimensions. The architect wants to convey a high sense of order as well as an emotional connection to space.

A number of perforated and differently sized stars puncture the exterior cantilevered eves, creating a dynamic play of light and shadow that changes through the course of the day in according to weather conditions. The exterior corridors and terrace encourage people to interact with one another, spaces vary as you move through the building, and views open up to the courtyard and beyond. The space between the buildings is as important as the buildings themselves.

In Ahmedabad, Gujarat, SPASM Design Architects have designed a dwelling which is a celebration of materiality and craftsmanship. The architect has integrated historical referenc-

es from his own lineage, yet remained modern in style while inheriting the characteristics of regionalism. D I Y A House has exhibited an extreme sensitivity to light and materials without becoming pastiche. Through the use of wooden louvres, the architecture plays with the natural light to create exciting spaces. In a sense, light is used as a building material which is sculpted. The sun is not excluded, but invited in via architectural elements.

The design utilizes modern planning and sensibilities, and local construction materials to create a contemporary yet regionalist dwelling. The ordering of open, private and intimate spaces demonstrates an understanding of the function of the building and the requirements of the family while retaining a connection with nature. Rustic and earthy vernacular colours and textures, combined with the material palette, create a totality of experience. Use of rusting Cor-ten steel on the exterior is consistent with the theme of textured patterning.[10]

D I Y A 주택에서는 독특한 재료를 능숙하게 어루만지는 장인의 솜씨가 느껴진다. 현대적인 건축물 속에 전통적인 요소를 녹여냄으로써 지역성을 드러내고 있기 때문이다. 전작과 마찬가지로 이 건물에서도 빛은 중요한 건축적 요소로 활용된다. 특히 목제 창살을 통해 내부로 끌어들인 빛은 공간을 더욱 흥미롭게 만든다. 그런 의미에서 보면 빛 역시 하나의 건축 재료로 볼 수 있지 않을까.

한편 지역적 재료로 현대적인 생활을 담아낸 공간 구성방식도 주목할 만하다. 개인 공간과 공용공간을 적절하게 여닫으며, 자연과의 관계를 유지하면서도 현대적 삶에 적합한 기능들을 모두 담아내고 있다. 이때 재료의 색과 질감은 모든 공간에 투박하면서도 소박한 일관적 분위기를 조성하며, 내부에서는 다양한 방식으로 사용되어 거주자들에게 풍성한 경험을 선사한다.

외부에 쓰인 내후성 강판은 현대적인 재료지만, 구멍을 뚫어 나무 문양을 새김으로써 독특한 분위기를 연출하고 있다. 이 작업에서는 나무와 건물이 맺고 있는 관계도 살펴볼 만하다. 부지 곳곳에 남겨진 나무들은 시원한 그늘을 드리우는 정원의 일부인 동시에, 자연 그 자체이기도 한 이유에서다. 이러한 공생은 인도 문화의 가장 근본적 특성 중 하나로, 이 사례에서는 정원의 나무들을 이용해 이 관계를 건축적으로 표현한다.

마지막으로 살펴볼 사례는 기원정사 불교 교육 센터다. 작업의 핵심은 대지의 기존 상태를 그대로 유지하는 것이다. 부지에 있던 나무를 단 한 그루도 베어내지 않기 위해 건물을 여섯 개의 동으로 분리해 나무 주변으로 배치했다. 그 과정에서 자연스레 두 개의 안뜰이 형성됐는데, 이는 여러 동의 건물을 하나로 엮어주는 연결고리 역할을 한다.

Jetavana Buddhist Learning Center, Sameep Padora and Associates

Colour is used in numerous architectural interior elements to enhance the experience of the building's depth and spatial qualities. There is diversity in interior elements and the architectural detailing, and an adaptation and referencing of the local vernacular in the use of perforated screens with patterns of trees and branches – a bow to the Sidi Saiyyed mosque Jaali. The relationship to trees, which provide essential shading and a continuous symbiosis with nature, is a fundamental aspect of Indian culture. In this project this relationship is emphasized by incorporating trees into the architectural space.[11] In Jetavana, a Buddhist Learning Centre designed by Studio Sameep Pedora and Associates is a flexible religious and cultural space used for festivals and community gatherings. The architect worked to a mandate of not harming a single tree on the site. The sizable program was split up into six buildings, each of them situated in gaps between the heavy planting. Through the design process two courtyards emerged as

links suturing these buildings into a common identity. There is a synthesis between inside outside, the utilization of local natural materials: rammed earth walls; basalt; a roof structure of repurposed timber finished with clay tiles and with an understructure of mud rolls; and traditional mud and dung flooring.

These buildings represent a sample of India's regionalist architecture – its identity, its values and its forms which reference modernist as well as vernacular characteristics. The projects accommodate the traditions of cultural continuity, and local and universal ideas. They constitute a bridge between the past and future, while providing a perspective on India's emerging architectural character. Gihan Karunaratne

이러한 배치가 장소성에서 비롯됐다면, 건물에 쓰인 재료들은 다분히 지역적이다. 벽과 바닥에 쓰인 진흙과 현무암, 구조체로 활용된 재활용 목재, 지붕을 덮은 흙 기와까지, 모두 인근에서 쉽게 구할 수 있는 재료들이다.

지금까지 소개한 다섯 개의 작품은 오늘날 인도 건축이 어떤 관점에서 지역성을 다루고 있는지 다양한 관점으로 개성 있게 보여준다. 인

도 건축의 전통, 종교를 아루르는 문화적 특징과, 한때 인도를 지배했던 근대 건축의 요소까지 고루 해석해 내면서 현대적인 특징도 적절히 담아내고 있다.

자신들의 문화를 바탕으로 하되, 이를 단순히 지역적인 관점으로만 국한시키지 않고 보편적인 가치로 확장하고 있다. 이렇듯 최근의 인도 건축은 과거와 미래 사이의 접점에 서서 변화의 새 물결을 일으키며 스스로 나아갈 새로운 방향을 제시하고 있다. 기한 카루나라튼

1. Sujata Keshavan, *Design and the Indian Identity*
2. Ivan R. Shumkov, *OOAc-CA 1.2. Globalization and critical regionalism*
3. Ranjith Dayaratne, "Critical Regionalism and the reconstruction of 'roots' in architecture"
4. A History of Architecture Critical Regionalism: Fine Arts sites, World Museums
5. Ar. Gaurav Gangwar 1 and Prabhjot Kaur, "Charles Correa: Seeking new Identity of Indian, Architecture through 'Critical Regionalism'"
   Zeenath Shakir, "Critical Regionalism", Archi blog, November 28, 2014
6. Ibid.
7. David Robson , *Beyond Bawa: Modern Masterworks of Monsoon Asia*, London, UK : Thames & Hudson, 2007
8. Kalpanee Jayatilake, "The Long House, Salvage modernism", The Architect, Vol 116, 2015
9. Nishan Wijetunge, "Architect The Salvage Dawg", The Architect, Vol 116, 2015
   Nishan Wijetunge, "Salvaging-Modus Operandi", The Architect, Vol 116, 2015
10. *Hirante Welandawe, HWA, Sri Lanka*, IABEDT
11. *Current work: Bijoy Jain, Studio Mumbai*, The Architectural League

Collage House
S+PS Architects

Living in Mumbai, India it is impossible to ignore the informal settlements in the city, and if looked at closely there are many lessons to be learnt in frugality, adaptability, multi-tasking, resourcefulness and ingenuity. A visual language emerges that is of the found object, ad-hoc, eclectic, patched and collaged. An attempt has been made here to apply some of these lessons without romanticizing or fetishizing them. The project looks at the idea of recycling and collage in several ways, from the very physical - like materials, energy, etc. to the intangible - like history, space and memories.

The front facade sets the tone for what lies within, with a "corner of windows" that recycles old windows and doors of demolished houses in the city. This becomes a major backdrop for the living room with a exposed concrete faceted ceiling above countered by the polished white marble with intricate brass inlay on the floor. Metal pipe leftovers pieced together like bamboo form a "pipe wall" integrating structural columns, rainwater downtake pipes and a sculpture of spouts that in the monsoon are a delight for all the senses. In the central courtyard on one side scrap rusted metal plates are riveted together, Kitsch colored tile samples retain a planter in the middle and on the third side is a wall clad in cut-waste stone slivers lifted off the back of stone cutting yards and waste generated on site. Hundred-year-old columns from a dismantled house bring back memories, and nostalgia is nourished with a lightweight, steel and glass pavilion (with solar panels

above) on the terrace level overlooking fabulous views down the hillside. This approach is reinforced again in the interior materials and elements. It plays up this contrast between the old and the new, the traditional and the contemporary, the rough and the finished. One finds use of recycled materials like old textile blocks, flooring out of old Burma teak rafters and purlins, colonial furniture, fabric waste (chindi) along with new ways of using traditional elements and materials like carved wooden mouldings, beveled mirrors, heritage cement tiles, etc.

A language emerges that is both new but strangely familiar at the same time and that makes us rethink notions of beauty that we take for granted around us. To make this mélange more "acceptable", it is encased in a "garb of modernity" (Nehru). This concrete frame - in a rough aggregate finish outside and in a smooth form finish inside - wraps and connects all the spaces from back to front and across all three levels.

To build on top of a hill is always exciting, until the architects discovered here that they were surrounded by neighbours on all sides. This led early on in the design process to look inwards and build around the quintessential Indian courtyard, albeit slightly modified. The court is actually raised a floor above the ground level and hidden below is a large rainwater harvesting tank wrapped with rock that was removed from the hillside during excavation. It is the core around which this large four-generation family is organized and comes together.

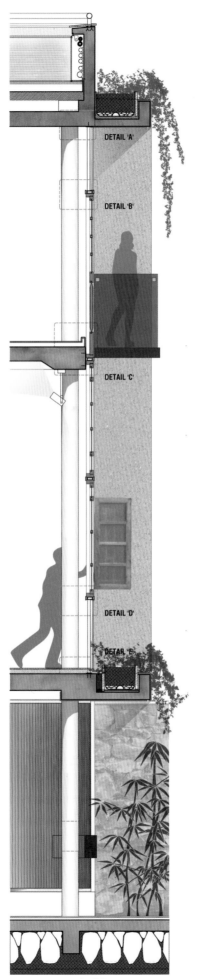

detail 1

1. R.C.C. SLAB
2. 10MM THK TOP BASE PLATE IN POSITION
3. 10MM Ø ANCHOR FASTNER HOLDING BASE PLATE IN POSITION GREY AGGREGATE PLASTER
4. ALUMINIUM CAP FOR POLYCARBONATE SHEET WITH EXTERNAL GRADE SILICONE SEALANT AT JOINT
5. 9" Ø M.S. COLUMN
6. 12MM THK MULTIWALL POLYCARBONATE SHEET
7. VERTICAL P.C. CLIP TO HOLD P.C. SHEETS
8. 1.5"X 1.5" M.S. BOX SECTION AS HANGER TO HOLD 1.5"X3" M.S. FRAME IN POSITION
9. 0.5" X 3.25" T.W. COVER MOULDING WITH 0.25"X0.25" GROOVE AT CENTRE
10. 1.5" X 3" M.S. FRAME MEMBER
11. 2" X 1" T.W. COVER MOULDING PATTI OVER 1.5" X 3" M.S. FRAME
12. RECYCLED T.W. WINDOW SHUTTER & PANEL/ GLASS
13. RECYCLED T.W. WINDOW FRAME
14. RECYCLED TIMBER FLOORING WITH SKIRTING AT END
15. 10MM THK WALL PLATE IN POSITION
16. STEPPED STONE CILL AS REBATE
17. 1-1/2" THK VERTICAL ROUGH CUDAPPAH PLANTER SIDE
18. EARTH FILLING
19. 10MM THK BOTTOM BASE PLATE
20. WATER PROOFING

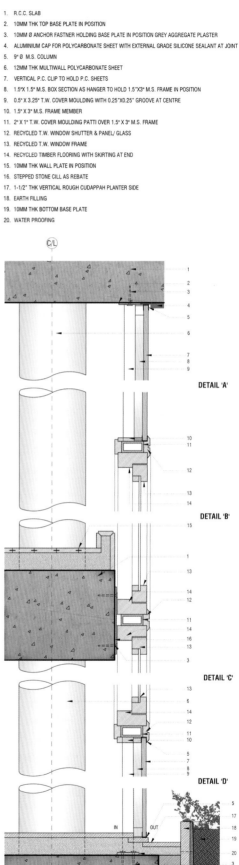

DETAIL 'A'

DETAIL 'B'

DETAIL 'C'

DETAIL 'D'

DETAIL 'E'

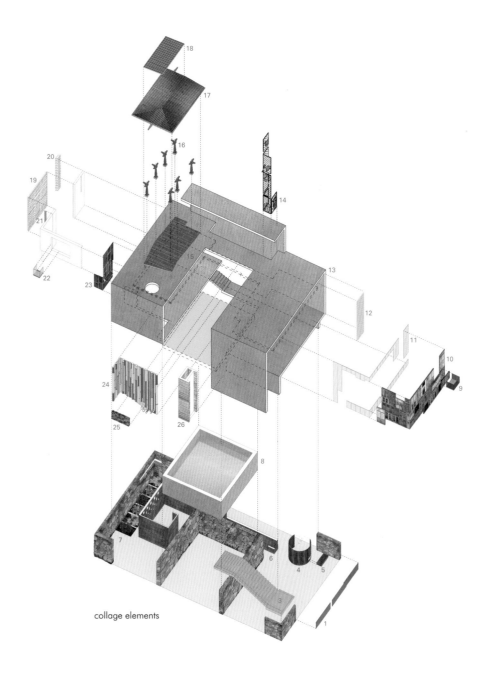

collage elements

1. corrugated metal shutters
2. walls of stone excavated from site
3. external stair from entry to courtyard
4. vertically stacked glass drum
5. M.S. plate box window in drum
6. exposed brick walls
7. organic farming planters
8. 50,000 liters rain water harvesting tank
9. blue glass balcony
10. recycled wooden windows curtain wall
11. multiwall frosted polycarbonate infill
12. aluminium plate louvers as screen
13. concrete envelope
14. metal mesh elevator enclosure
15. rough finish granite platform of pavilion
16. 100 year old wooden columns of pavilion
17. stainless steel roof over pavilion
18. solar panels on roof
19. treated bamboo screen on south side
20. wired glass louvers
21. projecting glass fin
22. yellow glass balcony
23. recycled metal plate cladding
24. recycled pipe wall
25. stub wall clad in tile sample
26. cladding out of waste stone stripes

rubblestone wall

brick masonary

fabric slab

faceted slab

faceted stair

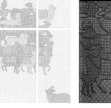

wasteplate wall

pipe wall

mesh enclosure

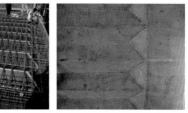

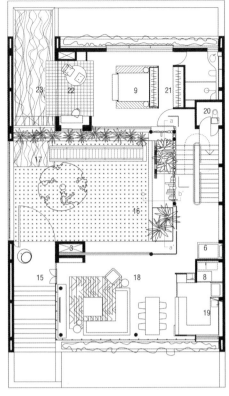

first floor

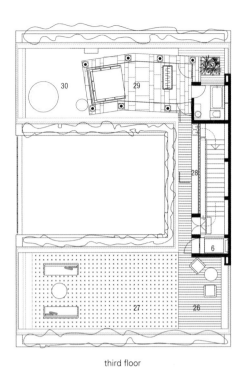

third floor

1. external stair to first floor 2. services 3. duct 4. parking
5. puja room 6. elevator 7. entry lounge 8. utility 9. bedroom
10. staff lobby 11. staff room 12. vegetable garden
13. 50,000L rain water harvesting tank 14. earth fill
15. veranda 16. courtyard 17. spillover pool 18. living-dining
19. kitchen 20. powder room 21. dressing 22. study
23. lap pool 24. pantry 25. balcony 26. deck 27. roof garden
28. counter 29. rooftop pavilion 30. dry landscape terrace

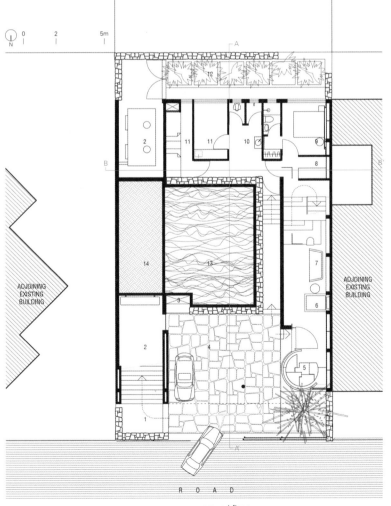

N   0   2   5m

ground floor

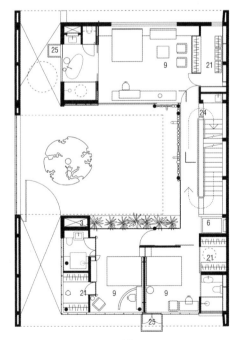

second floor

Project: Collage House / Location: Parsik Hill, Belapur, Navi Mumbai / Architects: S+PS Architects / Project team: Pinkish Shah, Shilpa Gore-Shah, Mayank Patel, Gaurav Agarwal, Shrutika Nirgun, Divya Malu, Manali Patel, Ved Panchwagh, Priyadarshi Srivastava / Liasion Architects: Sopan Prabhu Architects / Structural Engineers: Rajeev Shah & Associates Services Consultants: Arkk Consultants / Landscape Consultants: S+PS Architects / Site Supervision: Amish Mistry Architect / Models: S+PS Architects Project Estimate: Withhold At Owners Request / Client: Mr. Bhargava / Site area: 351m² / Gross floor area: 520m² / Design: 2006 / Completion: 2015

꼴라주 주택

인도 최대의 상업도시인 뭄바이는 빛과 그늘을 동시에 지닌 도시다. 고층 건물로 가득한 화려한 도심부에서 조금만 벗어나면 생존마저도 위협받는 아시아 최대의 슬럼가가 자리하고 있기 때문이다. 슬럼가의 집들은 90% 이상이 불법으로 지어졌기에 생활 환경은 무척 열악하지만, 그 속에도 삶의 지혜는 녹아있기 마련이다. 최소한의 비용으로 최대의 효과를 거두는 방법, 주어진 환경에 적응하는 방법, 그리고 이러한 상황 속에서도 자신만의 삶의 공간을 만드는 방법 등이다. 뿐만 아니라 그때그때 구한 각양각색의 재료를 덧붙이고 덜어내고 매만지는 과정을 거치다 보면, 때로는 철저한 계획하에 지어진 건물들과는 사뭇 다른 매력을 풍기기도 한다. 이 주택은 바로 이러한 점에 착안해 '재활용'과 '꼴라주'라는 키워드를 실험해본 작업이다.

꼴라주 기법이 가장 적극적으로 활용된 부분은 건물의 정면부다. 철거된 건물들에서 나온 수십 개의 창과 문을 이어붙여 세상에 하나뿐인 독특한 벽을 만든 것이다. 세월의 흔적을 오롯이 간직한 이 벽은 외부에서 봤을 때도 흥미롭지만, 내부공간에서도 제 몫을 톡톡히 한다. 노출 콘크리트와 유리, 대리석 등 현대적인 재료를 사용해 자칫 단조롭게 느껴질 수 있었던 거실에 생동감을 불어넣고 있기 때문이다.

독특한 분위기의 거실을 지나 계단실 쪽으로 가면 이번에는 대나무를 닮은 벽이 눈길을 사로잡는다. 각기 다른 굵기의 파이프를 조각내고 이어붙여 대나무처럼 보이게 만든 것인데 이 역시 버려진 파이프를 재활용했다.

무더운 열대지방의 기후를 고려해 건물 가운데는 널찍한 중정도 두었다. 중정에서는 입면에 사용됐던 꼴라주 기법이 한층 더 적극적으로 사용됐다. 투명한 유리, 대나무 모양의 파이프, 코르텐 철판, 그리고 철망까지, 중정을 둘러싼 네 개의 벽이 모두 다른 모습을 하고 있다. 색색의 타일을 조합해 만든 화분마저도 또 하나의 작은 콜라주 같다. 건물 곳곳에서 드러나는 키치적인 요소는 옥상에도 있다. 백 년의 세월을 간직한 고풍스러운 기둥을 활용해 주변 풍경을 즐길 수 있는 파빌리온을 만든 것이다. 오래된 기둥들은 유리와 철이라는 현대적인 재료를 만나 다시금 생명력을 갖게 된다.

이렇듯 이 집은 폐자재와 오래된 가구, 예스러운 장식들을 적극적으로 활용하고 있다. 동시에 건물 전체를 콘크리트 프레임으로 감싸 안음으로써 이러한 요소들이 단순히 과거에 머물지 않도록 했다. 그 결과 옛것과 새것, 전통과 현대를 조화롭게 녹여내면서, 새로우면서도 친숙한 아름다움이란 무엇인지를 보여준다.

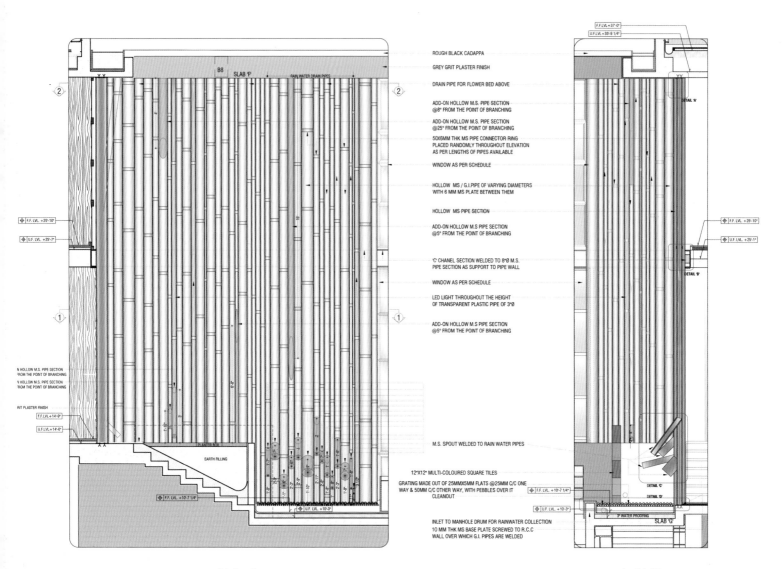

detail a-a'

detail b-b'

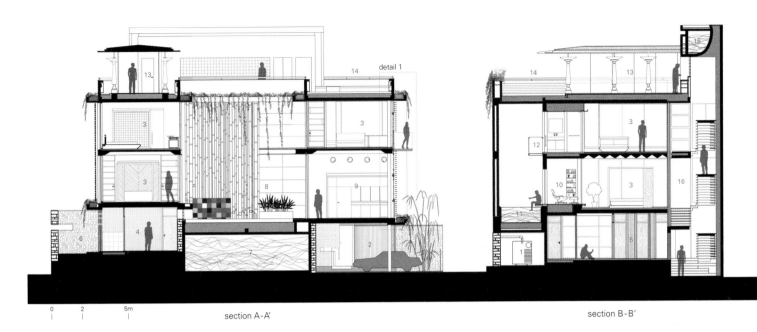

section A-A'   section B-B'

0   2   5m

1. services 2. parking 3. bedroom 4. staff lobby 5. staff room 6. vegetable garden 7. 50,000L rain water harvesting tank
8. courtyard 9. living-dining 10. study 11. lap pool 12. balcony 13. rooftop pavilion 14. dry landscape terrace 15. overhead tank 16. stairwell

DIYA House
SPASM Design Architects

Ahmedabad is predominantly dry through the year, though it does rain occasionally during monsoon months, from late June to August. The clients, a young couple with a daughter of 9 and their parents, contacted us for a family home. Named after their daughter "D I Y A" meaning the light that enlightens, this home we are certain will be loved and nurtured. Pre-existing trees and a large lawn, prompted the exact

positioning of the built form, the lower level, weaves spaces around trees, retaining all 284 of them. Several foundations were carefully positioned and hand dug to preserve roots, and the trees became generators of specific vistas and open to sky courtyards resulting in a formless labyrinth of interconnected spaces.

Arrival is announced by a 16 meters column free span canopy,

which creates a 2.4 meters high entry space, bound by vertical pivoting wooden louvers. This filter like space allows breezes to freely flow through to the main courtyard beyond, and frames an existing Neem tree as a sculpture, a powerful presence of nature is sensed throughout the house.

The architecture deploys different strategies, to mitigate the intense heat.

An organic plan, bound by Massive rammed earth walls with high thermal mass, and courtyards (preserving trees), vertical pivoting wooden louvers, top hung windows with mesh inserts keeps out mosquitoes and allows breezes/breathing. Aided by giant sliding glass walls, which retract into pockets, the living, dining spaces seamlessly connect with the surrounding verdant environment. Shade from the upper

cantilever storey brings respite and is welcoming in this tropical region.

Apart from these measures, sprinklers activate on timers to
humidify the courts which are all planted with Ferns, Mon-
steras, Allocasias, Philodendrons, Rafis palms, Terminalias and
other plant species.

The upper storey is resolved with a skin of Corten, each single
element of 0.5 meters x 5.5 meters high panels which hang
off the internal structure, creating a ventilated facade to again

absorb the heat from the incident sun and release upwards
vide air circulation behind them hence reducing heat gain of
the inner structure and spaces.

The corners of the volume are perforated as Jaalis in the patterns of trees and branches, a bow to the Sidi Saiyyed Mosque
Jaali, an architectural wonder of Ahmedabad. These spaces
become dappled in patterned light and shade, along with the
sliding screens on the principal eye of the facade, cooling the
breezes through the venturi effect of the Jaali screens.

Over deck foam insulation coupled with reflective glazed tiles, sliding screens, giant Agassi (balcony) spaces and the ventilated Corten facade, all work in unison to reduce heat gain. The forthcoming nature of the clients led to the design of an entire series of furniture and objects specifically for their home. These were all designed in 20mm x 20mm brass sections and salvaged wood. Mirrors, towel racks, book shelves, vanities, TV stands, occasional tables, nest of trays were all designed as bespoke objects.

The main staircase to the upper level is an assemblage of thick wood akin to a stack in a drying yard, the stair rail is crafted out of rosewood as a precious object with the bent corners of cast brass, pronouncing an elegant luxury along with a sense of timelessness.

Throughout the project – the level of craftsmanship is exquisite. All the ART is gifted to the clients by friends and family.

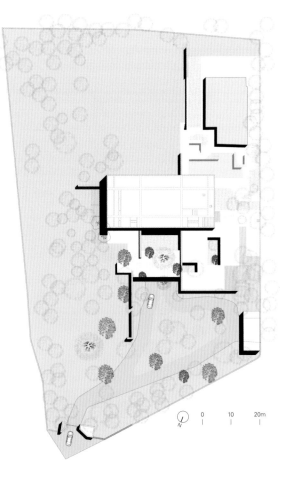

0   10   20m

DIYA 주택

인도 서부에 있는 아마다바드 시는 연중 건조한 편이지만, 7월 말부터 8월까지는 가끔 비가 내리는 우기이다. 이곳에, 9살 딸을 가진 젊은 부부가 부모님과 함께 살 집을 의뢰하였다. '깨달음으로 이르는 빛'이라는 의미를 지닌 딸의 이름을 그대로 가져와 명명한 집은 사랑과 온정이 가득할 것이다.

기존의 나무들과 잔디밭을 고려하여 건물의 형태가 결정되었다. 284 그루나 되는 나무를 모두 그대로 보존하기 위해 나무 사이 사이로 집이 들어설 자리를 결정했다. 더 나아가, 건물의 기초도 뿌리를 건드리지 않도록 세심하게 계획되었으며, 심지어 굴착 작업도 최대한의 손상을 피하고자 일일이 손으로 이루어졌다. 덕분에 부지의 수목들은 미로같이 얽힌 공간 속에서 각기 독특한 풍경을 간직하며 안뜰을 향해 열린다.

입구에는 기둥 없이 돌출된 16m 폭의 캐노피가 그늘을 만든다. 2.4미터 높이의 이 진입 공간을, 목제 미늘살이 수직으로 창을 이루며 두른다. 여과 장치 같은 이 공간은 바람이 자유롭게 흐를 뿐 아니라, 기존

Project: D I Y A / Location: Ahmedabad, Gujarat, India / Architects: SPASM Design Architects / Project architect: Divyesh Kargathra / Project team: Sangeeta Merchant, Divyesh Kargathra, Gauri Satam, Mansoor Ali Kudalkar, Sanjeev Panjabi / Site supervision: Haresh Patel, Ramdev, Sandesh Pawar / Structural engineer: Gmr consultants /

의 수목들을 강조하며 자연의 조형미를 건물 전체로 끌어들인다.

주택은 다양한 방식으로 이 지역의 강렬한 열기를 식힌다. 우선, 많은 열을 흡수할 수 있는 거대한 흙벽을 활용해 공간을 유기적으로 조직했다. 여기에는 수목들을 그대로 보존한 안뜰과 함께, 수직 목재 미늘창과 들창을 곳곳에 배치하여 바람이 쉽게 불어 들어올 수 있도록 했다. 모기나 해충을 막기 위해 방충망도 별도로 설치했다.

전면 유리 창호는 미닫이로 만들어, 거실과 식사실이 주변의 녹지 환경을 향해 완전히 열린다. 돌출된 위층이 만들어내는 그늘은 열대기후에 꼭 필요한 휴식처를 제공해준다. 이 외에도 살수 장치를 설치해 건물 곳곳의 뜰에 심어진 식물들에 수분을 공급한다.

2층을 마감하는 내후성 강판은 벽체와 간격을 두어 공기층을 형성해 자연 환기를 할 수 있다. 이 덕분에 외부에서 흡수된 태양열은 다시 내부의 공기 순환에 기여하여 집안 기온을 낮춘다.

건물의 모서리는 구멍 뚫린 강판으로 장식했다. 각종 나뭇가지 모양으로 구멍을 뚫어 만든 문양은 인근의 전통 건축 유산을 참조한 것이다. 이 가림막을 통해 아름다운 빛과 그림자는 시원한 바람과 함께 들어온다.

발포 단열재와 더불어, 커다란 실외 테라스를 쾌적하게 식히기 위해 반사 유리로 바닥재를 마감했다. 여기에 미닫이 가림막과 구멍 뚫린 내후성 강판도 냉각 효과에 기여한다.

내부의 가구와 공간 소품도 맞춤형으로 제작했다. 모두 황동 부재와 재활용 목재를 재료로 만들었다. 거울, 수건 선반, 서재 서가, 화장대, 탁자, 그리고 쟁반에 이르기까지 모두 수작업으로 만들었다.

2층으로 오르는 주 계단도 독특한 방식으로 계획했다. 두꺼운 목재를 마치 벌채 건조장에서 말리기 위해 쌓아 올린 형태로 만들었다. 난간은 자단 나무로 제작했으며, 끝은 황동으로 둥글게 마무리되어 우아한 고전미를 드러낸다.

주택 작업 전체는 정교하고 능숙한 솜씨로 완성되었다. 친구들과 가까운 친지들에게 선물 받은 예술품들도 우아한 내부 분위기를 만드는 데 한몫을 했다.

MEP: MEP consulting engineers / Rammed earth wall construction: Hunnarshala Foundation / Corten ventilated facade and perforated screens: Phenix Construction Technologies / Out sourced furniture: Sources unlimited / Specialist lighting: vis a vis india pvt.ltd. / Audio visual consultant: The soundsmiths / Sanitaryware: FCML India / Landscape: GSA (Green Space Alliance) / Carpenters: Krishna Interiors / Electricals: Rajubhai Power Control / Site area: 10,930m² / Bldg. area: 2,470m² / Design: 2010 / Construction: 2011 / Completion: 2016 / Photograph: ©Sebastian Zachariah (courtesy of the architect)

detail 1

balcony   living area   balcony

living area

0   2   5m

section A-A'

1. corten panel in varying widths - Panel to be made in 'L' angle frame on all 4 sides of size 75mm x 75mm and clad in 1.6mm thk. corten sheet and the panel to be hung on 75mm x 50mm 'T' cleats to be fixed on wall with 15 mm dia rod x 50mm wide
2. ceiling to be clad in 4mm thk. veneer and finished in monocoat
3. corten fixed Jaali panel to be fixed on to top and bottom panel with bolts
4. corten Jaali panel on to sliding chanels

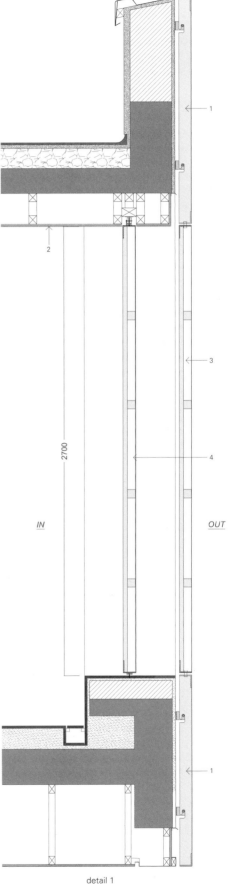

detail 1

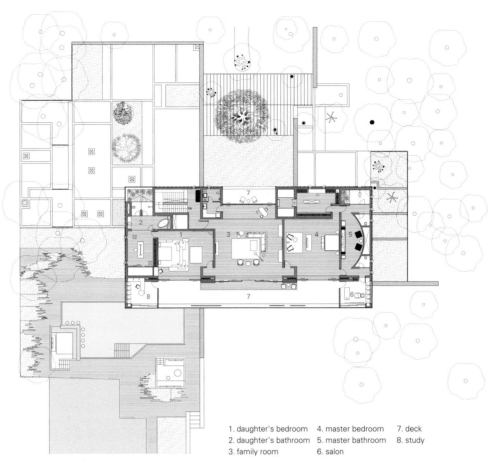

1. daughter's bedroom   4. master bedroom   7. deck
2. daughter's bathroom   5. master bathroom   8. study
3. family room   6. salon

first floor

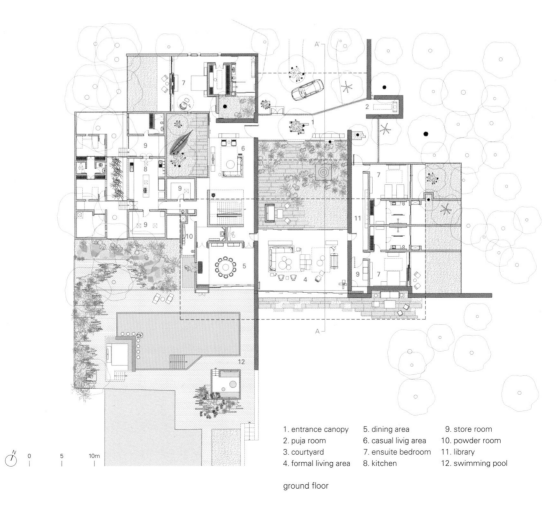

1. entrance canopy   5. dining area   9. store room
2. puja room   6. casual livig area   10. powder room
3. courtyard   7. ensuite bedroom   11. library
4. formal living area   8. kitchen   12. swimming pool

ground floor

Riparian House

Architecture Brio

We called the project "The Riparian House" since we imagined the house as an organism living on the edge of the water. The house is built inside the earth to stay cool naturally, situated just below the top of the hillock so that it can overlook its surrounding. It gives the river landscape a sense of scale and drama. We like to work with this confrontation between the "man-made" and "nature".

The river on which the house is located is perennial and flows down from the mountainous landscape of the Western Ghats. During the monsoons the water level can rise about two meters. Along the river banks in the low lying areas there are mostly small agrarian fields, which yield quite a few crops due to the availability of water. However the land which is located at a higher level changes from a dense brightly green coloured jungle-like forest during the monsoon months to a pale brown shrubby wasteland during the dry and hot summer months. Water-intensive lawns on the property are therefore kept to a minimal. The plantation of drought tolerant fountain grasses mitigates this transition to a dry landscape, while also relating to the riparian landscape that exists along the river.

This pastoral scenery is bound to change very quickly though.

Mumbai was earlier confined to the island city. But since it's crossed the bay is rapidly expanding into its agricultural backyard. Houses like this are a precursor to the phenomena of urbanisation. But more often than not, what's being built are glaringly abundant trophy houses for the rich urban middle class, attempting to establish itself with looming boundary walls into the landscape as the new landlords.

The separation between "untouched" nature and "man-made" nature is rather unclear in most rural landscapes around India where habitation is close. The landscape surrounding the house is neither used as agricultural, nor is it untouched. Often cattle comes grazing or branches of trees are used for fodder. It has a jungle like appearance but human activity is rather intense.

Nature is not something passive, something just to be viewed. In a rapidly urbanising India, nature and its natural discomforts tend to increasingly get shut off from the daily experience. The purpose of a home in a setting like Karjat is to reimagine the relationship of oneself with nature. While this often leads to an architecture which attempts to blur the boundaries between inside and outside or tries to mimic nature itself, our aim was to emphasize the confrontation between architecture and nature as well.

A master bedroom, bathroom, dining and living area sit along the front, a more open face of the house. Both the living room in the western corner of the house and the master bedroom in the northern corner enjoy panoramic views to the river.

The kitchen occupies a central position along with the open to sky courtyard and is flanked on either side by two bedrooms at the two far ends. These spaces are embedded in the earth with windows brining in ample light from above and the river side.

Galvanized steel mullioned windows break down the scale of the front façade of the house. A rhythmic row of bamboo poles is placed at close intervals in front of the house to create a layer of privacy without obstructing the spectacular view of the river and the mountains beyond.

The building has to respond to these extreme conditions by allowing enough shade and breeze during the summer and providing a waterproof indoor environment during the stormy monsoons. The screen of bamboos creates an ever-changing pattern of light and shadow throughout the seasons and times of the day, making the building a 'sensor' of light.

The walls are built in Indian limestone in a coarsed pattern, which make the house seem to rise out of the ground giving it a solid base. This is contrasted by the lightness of a suspended timber deck verandah which surrounds the house on three sides. The covered verandahs allow for comfortably ventilated and shaded semi-indoor spaces. Internally the timber floor continuous as a border around various patterned natural stone floors. In front of the living room the deck extends to form a large outdoor deck with a panoramic view of the surrounding landscape. Robert Verrijt

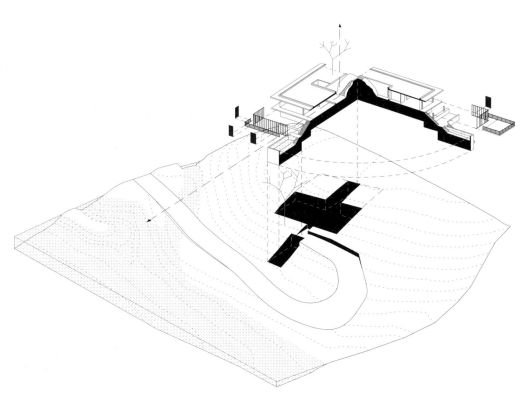

언덕바지 작은 집

집은 고요히 흐르는 강물과 맞닿은 곳에서 숨을 품는다. 언덕바지 바로 아래에, 대지의 선선한 기운을 간직하며 주변을 향해 열린다. 풍경은 새로운 이야기를 만들어내기 시작한다. 이렇듯 자연과 인간이 손을 맞잡고 독특한 공간을 만든다.

집은 서쪽의 구릉지대에서부터 연중 흘러 내려오는 강을 끼고 있다. 우기에는 수위가 무려 2미터까지 오르기도 한다. 강둑 너머 저지대에는 작은 경작지들이 여기저기 흩어져있다. 물과 인접하기에 꽤 많은 수확을 거둔다. 그러나 조금 더 높은 지대는 기후의 영향을 받아 확연히 다른 모습으로 바뀐다. 비가 많은 계절에는 짙고 푸르른 우림이었다가, 고온의 마른 계절에는 옅은 고동 관목들이 우거진 황야가 된다. 이 때문에 부지에는 물을 많이 필요로 하는 잔디가 최소로 조성되었다. 대신에, 강수량이 적은 건기에도 잘 견디는 다년초를 곳곳에 심었다. 이는 강변 식생 환경과도 유사하다.

이 한가로운 전원 풍경은 그러나 곧 급격하게 변할 지도 모른다. 인근의 대도시 뭄바이는 한 때 섬에만 국한되었으나, 이제는 내륙의 만으로까지 급속히 확대되어 농경지대까지 후퇴시키고 있다. 도시화 현상과 함께 점차 많은 주택들이 교외에 지어지고 있지만, 대부분의 경우는 부유한 중산층들을 위한 화려한 전유물로, 높은 담장을 치며 풍경의 새 주인 노릇을 한다.

인도 교외에서도 아주 외진 지역에서는 본연 그대로의 자연과 거주지의 인위 환경 사이의 경계가 명확하지 않다. 여기서 자연은 그저 바라보기 위한 대상만이 아니다. 집들을 둘러싸는 자연은 경작지로 다듬어져 있지 않지만, 그렇다고 아예 방치된 것도 아니다. 줄곧 소들의 방목지가 되거나, 꺾어 모은 수풀은 가축의 먹이가 된다. 비록 밀림처럼 우거져 보일지라도 인간 활동은 비교적 활발하게 이루어진다.

그러나 도시화가 급속히 진행되는 인도에서는, 자연과 이에 당연히 뒤따르는 불편함은 점점 더 일상 생활에서 괴리되고 있다. 그래서 이 집은 독특한 자연 환경에서 주변 풍경과 새로운 관계를 찾고자 한다. 이 때문에 때로는 안과 밖이 모호해지기도 하며, 공간은 자연을 곧이곧대로 따라 하기도 한다. 하지만 어떠한 경우에도 건축은 자연과 마주하며 대응한다.

주침실과 화장실, 식사실과 거실은 밖을 향해 열려있다. 특히 서측 모서리의 거실 공간과, 북측 모서리의 주침실 공간에서는 강을 향한 풍경이 넓게 펼쳐진다. 부엌 공간은 하늘을 향해 열린 작은 뜰과 함께, 집의 중심을 이룬다. 여기서 두 개의 침실 공간은 양측 끝에 배치된다. 대지 안에 깊숙이 자리잡고 있지만 천창을 통해, 그리고 반대편의 강변을 향해 열려 있는 창들을 통해 충분한 빛을 들인다.

주택 전면의 아연 도금 강 창호는 공간의 전체 규모를 한결 낮춘다. 곳곳에 대나무로 얼기설기 세워 만든 가림벽은 언덕과 강으로 아우러진 풍경을 헤치지 않으면서도 불필요한 시선을 차단한다. 시간과 계절에 따라 끊임없이 변하는 그림자를 아로새기며 공간을 빛으로 정교하게 장식한다.

건물은 여름에는 충분한 그늘과 바람을 들이고, 호우에는 완전히 닫힌다. 이러한 공간 장치는 내·외부 사이에 흥미로운 관계를 형성하는 동시에, 때로는 극적으로 변하는 주변 자연환경에도 대응한다.

주택의 벽체는 인도의 석회암 석재로 거칠게 쌓아 올려, 마치 대지로부터 견고하게 솟아오른 듯한 인상을 준다. 이는 주택의 세 면에서 튀어나와 가볍게 떠있는 듯한 목제 실외 테라스와 대조를 이룬다. 돌출된 지붕 처마로 덮인 이 외부 공간에는 바람이 흐르고 그늘이 드리워진다. 실내는 나무 바닥이 천연 석재 바닥들 사이를 누비며 집 전체로 이어진다. 한편, 거실은 실외 테라스까지 확장되면서 주변 전경을 안으로 끌어들인다. 로버트 베리잇

Project: The Riparian House
Location: Karjat, Maharasthra, India
Architects: Architecture BRIO
Design team: Robert Verrijt, Shefali Balwani, Sahil Deshpande, Shuba Shekar, Prajakta Gawde
Landscape design: Architecture BRIO
Contractor: Raj Construction
Bldg. area: 330m²
Completion: 2015.10
Photograph: ©Ariel Huber / EDIT images (courtesy of the architect)

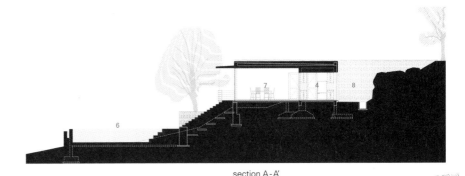

section A-A'

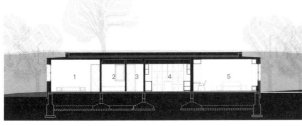

section B-B'

1. kid's room 2. staff bathroom 3. pantry 4. kitchen 5. guest bedroom
6. pool 7. dining room 8. kitchen courtyard 9. deck 10. living room
11. guest bedroom 12. guest bathroom

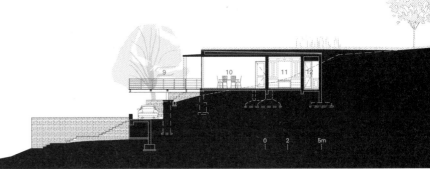

section C-C'

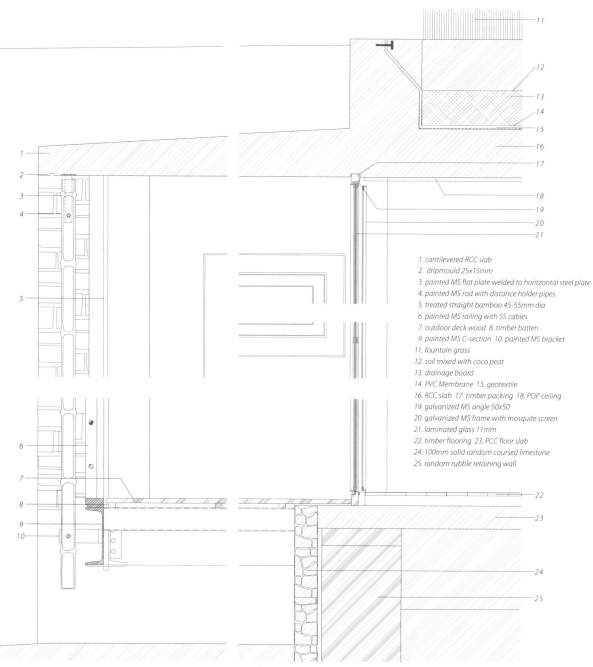

1. cantilevered RCC slab
2. dripmould 25x15mm
3. painted MS flat plate welded to horitzontal steel plate
4. painted MS rod with distance holder pipes
5. treated straight bamboo 45-55mm dia
6. painted MS railing with SS cables
7. outdoor deck wood 8. timber batten
9. painted MS C-section 10. painted MS bracket
11. fountain grass
12. soil mixed with coco peat
13. drainage board
14. PVC Membrane 15. geotextile
16. RCC slab 17. timber packing 18. POP ceiling
19. galvanized MS angle 50x50
20. galvanized MS frame with mosquite screen
21. laminated glass 11mm
22. timber flooring 23. PCC floor slab
24. 100mm solid random coursed limestone
25. random rubble retaining wall

detail section a-a'

Jetavana Buddhist Learning Center

Sameep Padora and Associates

In Buddhist mythology Jetvana is the name of the Buddha's most important spatial edifice which when literally translated means: the grove of Jeta, land donated to the sangha for founding a monastery. It was of semiotic significance that the site offered by Samir Somaiya owner of the neighboring sugar factory in rural Maharashtra for the Buddhist Learning Center was thickly forested, an idyllic grove of sorts.

The institute was programmed as a spiritual & skill development center for the native Dalit Bauddha Ambedkar Buddhist community. The mandate of Jetavana is to provide a spiritual anchor for their practice of Buddhist thought through meditation and yoga while also imparting training and skill development for members of the community.

With the mandate of not harming a single tree on site the sizable program was split up into 6 buildings each situated in gaps between the heavy planting. Through the design process two courtyards emerged as links suturing these buildings into a common identity.

Further by inverting the roof profile with a center valley in the middle and rising edges the interior spaces were visually connected with the foliage outside. The interior spaces hence are also a function of the outside setting, with a lightness that belies the heavy programs on site. The separation of the roof from the walls while providing much needed cross ventilation also scales the building towards the courtyard.

Working closely with Hunnarshala, an institution looking to revive and resuscitate local building traditions we collated a material palate that uses rammed load-bearing walls of basalt stone dust. The stone dust, which is waste from a nearby quarry, is mixed with waste fly ash, a by-product from the

adjoining factory that in the past was paying people to cart the waste fly ash away. Repurposed wood from old shipping vessels act as roof structure, with the understructure made of mud rolls, which are also great insulation. The roof itself is finished with clay roof tiles, remnants from older demolished buildings.

The flooring is a traditional mud and dung floor done by members of the local community, which is known to have antiseptic properties.

Our approach to the Jetavana project looks to extend the idea of the regional paradigm whilst separating it from the pervasive 'image' of what defines the local. The construction process also sets out an approach that looks to further construction techniques based on local materiality not necessarily used natively but appropriate for it's context.

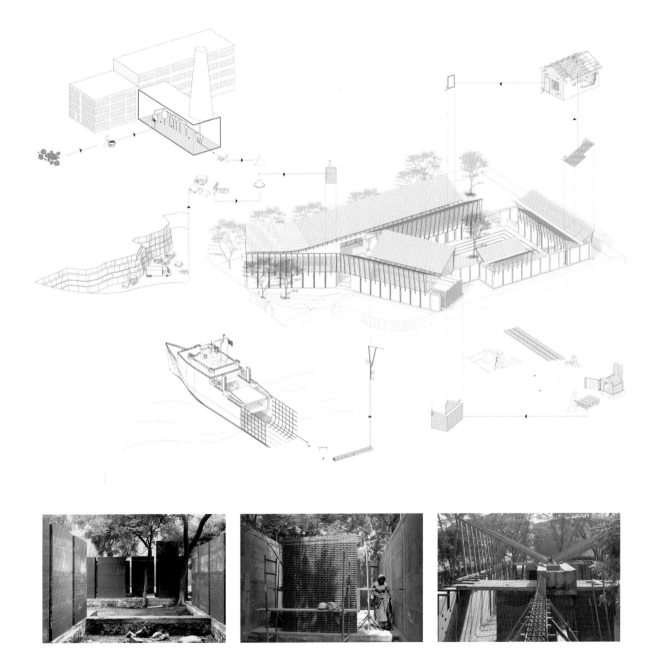

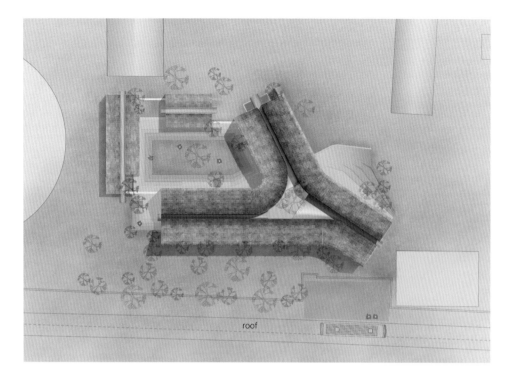

roof

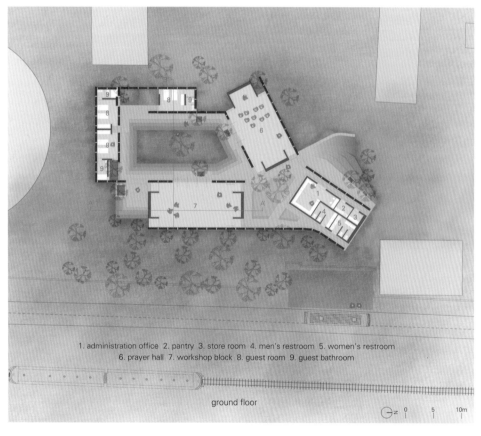

1. administration office 2. pantry 3. store room 4. men's restroom 5. women's restroom
6. prayer hall 7. workshop block 8. guest room 9. guest bathroom

ground floor

N   0   5   10m

Project: Jetavana / Location: Sakarwadi, Maharashtra, India / Architects: sP+a (Sameep Padora and Associates) / Design team: Sameep Padora, Karan Bhatt, Kriti Veerappan, Aparna Dhareshwar / Construction team: Soudagar Kulal, Atul Kulkarni / Structural design: Rajiv Shah / Artisan consultants and coordinators: Hunnarshala (Kiran Vaghela, Tejas Kotak, Bharat Chauhan, Hemant Dudhaiya) / Project managers and site supervision: Saudagar Kudal, Atul Kulkarni / Client: Somaiya Trust
Site area: 1,500m² / Bldg. area: 750m² / Materials: foundation (locally procured basalt stone, plinth (earth filled), floor (mud and cowdung plaster), walls (rammed quarry dust-flyash, ceramic tiles in restroom areas, exposed Bricks), roof understructure (salvaged Seasoned wood from ship breaking yard), roof finish (recycled and locally procured mangalore tiles), doors and windows (mosquito mesh with wooden frames), lights and ceiling fans (locally procured fittings)
Construction: 2014 / Completion: 2016.1 / Photograph: ©Edmund Sumner (courtesy of the architect)

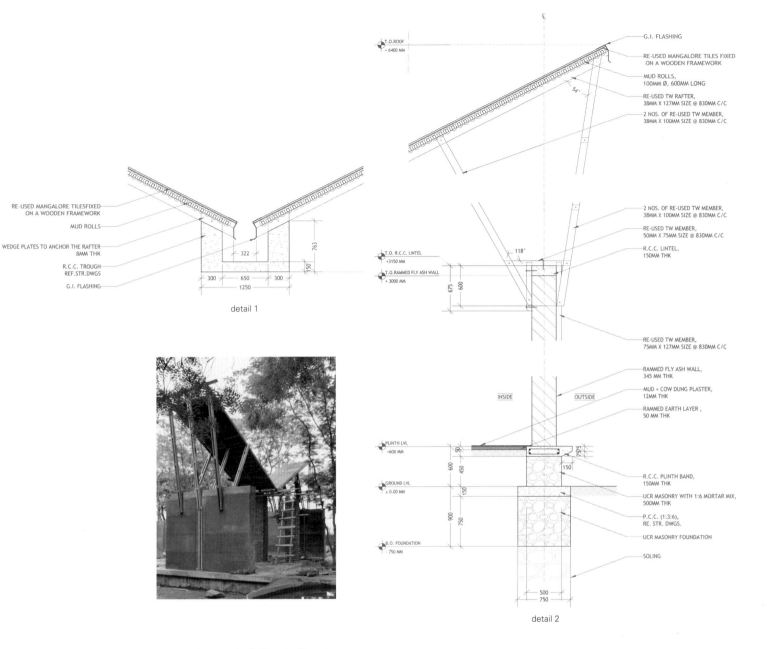

detail 1

RE-USED MANGALORE TILESFIXED ON A WOODEN FRAMEWORK

MUD ROLLS

WEDGE PLATES TO ANCHOR THE RAFTER 8MM THK

R.C.C. TROUGH REF.STR.DWGS

G.I. FLASHING

322
763
150
300 650 300
1250

G.I. FLASHING

RE-USED MANGALORE TILES FIXED ON A WOODEN FRAMEWORK

MUD ROLLS, 100MM Ø, 600MM LONG

RE-USED TW RAFTER, 38MM X 127MM SIZE @ 830MM C/C

2 NOS. OF RE-USED TW MEMBER, 38MM X 100MM SIZE @ 830MM C/C

T.O.ROOF +6400 MM

54°

2 NOS. OF RE-USED TW MEMBER, 38MM X 100MM SIZE @ 830MM C/C

RE-USED TW MEMBER, 50MM X 75MM SIZE @ 830MM C/C

R.C.C. LINTEL, 150MM THK

T.O. R.C.C. LINTEL +3150 MM

T.O.RAMMED FLY ASH WALL +3000 MM

118°

675
600

RE-USED TW MEMBER, 75MM X 127MM SIZE @ 830MM C/C

RAMMED FLY ASH WALL, 345 MM THK

MUD + COW DUNG PLASTER, 12MM THK

RAMMED EARTH LAYER, 50 MM THK

INSIDE   OUTSIDE

PLINTH LVL +600 MM

50
600
450
150
75
150

R.C.C. PLINTH BAND, 150MM THK

UCR MASONRY WITH 1:6 MORTAR MIX, 500MM THK

GROUND LVL ± 0.00 MM

900
750

P.C.C. (1:3:6), RE. STR. DWGS.

UCR MASONRY FOUNDATION

B.O. FOUNDATION -750 MM

SOLING

500
750

detail 2

기원정사 불교 교육 센터

기원전 6세기경, 인도 스리바스티 지역에 지어진 기원정사는 부처가 가장 오랜 시간 머물렀던 사원으로 잘 알려져 있다. 불교 역사상 두 번째로 기록될 만큼 유서 깊은 이 사원은 건립 배경에 얽힌 일화로도 유명하다. 당시 이 부지는 코살라국의 왕자인 기타의 소유였는데, 부처의 가르침에 감화된 스리바스티의 부호 급고독장자는 이곳에 부처를 위한 사원을 짓고자 했다. 이에 왕자는 이 땅을 모두 금으로 채운다면 땅을 팔겠노라 약속했고, 부호는 자신의 전 재산을 바쳐 땅을 금으로 덮어 결국 사원을 지었다는 이야기다.

최근 이러한 기원정사의 이름을 딴 불교 교육 센터가 인도 서부 마하라시트라 주에 완공됐다. 그 옛날의 기원정사처럼, 지역 주민들이 부처의 가르침을 되새기며 몸과 마음을 수양할 수 있도록 이 지방에서 설탕 공장을 운영하는 사업가의 기부로 지어진 시설이다.

주민을 위한 공간인 만큼 작업은 지역성에 초점을 맞춰 이뤄졌다. 지역의 전통적인 건축기술로, 주변에서 구할 수 있는 재료를 활용해, 부지의 기존 상황을 훼손하지 않은 채 건물을 짓고자 한 것이다.

이러한 태도는 건물의 배치에서부터 명확하게 드러난다. 울창한 숲 속에 자리잡은 건물은 총 여섯 개의 동으로 이루어지는데, 기능별로 분절된 각 건물은 부지에 있던 나무들을 피해서 들어선다. 모든 생명을 귀하게 여긴 부처의 뜻을 따르듯 단 한 그루의 나무도 베어내지 않은 것이다. 동시에 이러한 배치로 인해 생겨난 두 개의 마당은 여러 개의 건물을 하나로 엮어주는 연결고리 역할을 한다.

센터에서 건축적으로 가장 흥미로운 요소는 역삼각형 모양의 지붕이다. 가운데가 뾰족하게 솟은 일반적인 박공지붕과는 달리, 지붕의 높이는 가장자리로 갈수록 점점 높아진다. 외벽과 지붕 사이에 생긴 틈 사이로 건물 안에서도 바깥 풍경을 즐길 수 있다. 견고한 벽이 안팎을 가르고 있음에도 내외부가 하나로 연결된듯한 느낌을 받게 되는 것이다. 중심의 움푹 파진 부분으로는 빗물이 흘러 자연 배수가 가능하다. 뿐만 아니라 이 틈새로 자연 환기도 이뤄져 내부 환경은 더욱 쾌적해진다.

지역색이 물씬 풍기는 재료들도 주목할 만하다. 먼저 건물의 뼈대에는 오래된 선박에 쓰였던 목재를, 지붕에는 철거된 건물에서 구한 진흙 타일을 재활용했다. 또한, 인근 채석장에서 나오는 폐기물인 현무암 가루를 섞어 구조벽을 만들었으며, 비교적 얇은 벽에는 진흙을 활용해 단열성을 높였다. 마지막으로 바닥은 진흙에 사람의 분변을 섞은 재료로 마감했는데 자연적인 살균 효과도 기대할 수 있다.

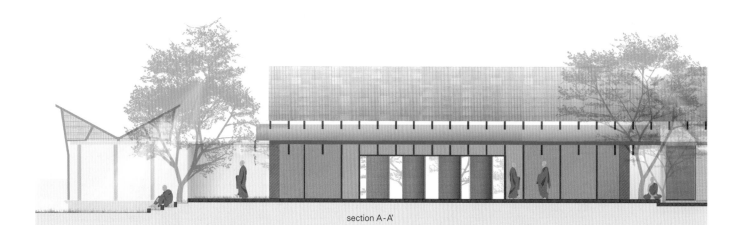

section A-A'

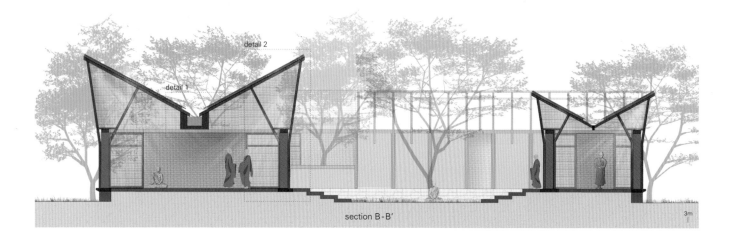

detail 2

detail 1

section B-B'

3m

National Institute for Faith Leadership

Archohm Consults

Envisaged as a tool to evolve and modernize Islam to make it relevant today, the National Institute of Faith Leadership campus reconnects the nationalist and liberal Islamic virtues and evolves the understanding of this faith; celebrating traditional values that are relevant to contemporary times. The students of this institute are the faith leaders of the future.

The building complex houses programmatic needs of this faith facility. Devoid of design as decoration, the spaces needed to evoke bare thought. Bold architectural impressions intended to push people towards brave expressions. Play of light in space and in time both brought in the required ethic and aesthetic to the institution.

The breaking of the arch is synonymous with the opening of the mind from myths and traditions. The iconic entrance is celebrating just that; an arch in concrete removes the 'key stone' to liberate the form, allowing in light and space. The basic form of this object on site is mass with a hole. A courtyard that allows light in to the building as it celebrates the introverted magnificence of an Islamic institution. The arch anchors the courtyard controlling the free flowing stone wall as the landscape respects the traditional geometry. The courtyard is positioned at mid-level to two floors of the institute so as to maximize access to nature, to light and green. The strong ascending stone wall wraps around the rigid form to bring in a certain dynamism to the external face. It encompasses a palm courtyard to protect and limit views of the reception space. It closes the center court and terminates into a winding courtyard of its own that facilitates a ramp that wraps across all floors to make the campus disabled friendly. This natural stonewall is another element that celebrates the traditional material in contemporary light.

The basic mass of brick is a simple set of classrooms, language laboratories and faculty spaces that are multi-functional. They open up to the courtyard with a wide verandah that works as a meeting and a sitting space. These spaces are as much a classroom as the traditional ones- One by discourse and the

other by debate. The entrance area is the reception, a floor of office below and the residence of the vice chancellor above. All spaces take in light through various light wells that allow a clean closed external mass, an expression of Islamic values. Two concrete volumes interface with the brick mass. They extrude and extend themselves out of the brick line to facilitate a slit of light and express as a mass that is further exaggerated by a large circular window. The two externally similar formal interventions are different in their internal function and thus accordingly adapt themselves spatially.

The library is a double height space with a large circle of light. The bare stone floors, wood structures and concrete walls, the double height stacks of books, the desktop multimedia library and the relaxed seating; all reflect a reflective learning space. The multipurpose hall on other side is a prayer hall, a collective gathering space and a place for large lectures. This volume is again bathed with light through a circle and a slit.

The floor below is a cool large dining hall that is punctuated by a semi-circular opening as a play of offset concrete walls to block views but allow light, a crescent light, again a reference to a dialogue between traditional and modern.

The entire mass is covered with a concrete cantilevered plane; an expression in plan of the breaking of the shell (the mind), as this overhanging protective shade of concrete shields and veils the campus, but opens up to the open arch. This floating floor on top is punctuated with star triangles with white and yellow renderings (a representation of geometric graphical Muslim motifs) that draw in a drama of forms and shades all over the internal courtyard across the day as a dialogue with the harsh sun.

This metaphoric play of stars on campus is intended to enchant and excite the mind on one side but more importantly distract it for the rigorous and regimented learning to balance the institution with flair of fun and freedom. Sourabh Gupta

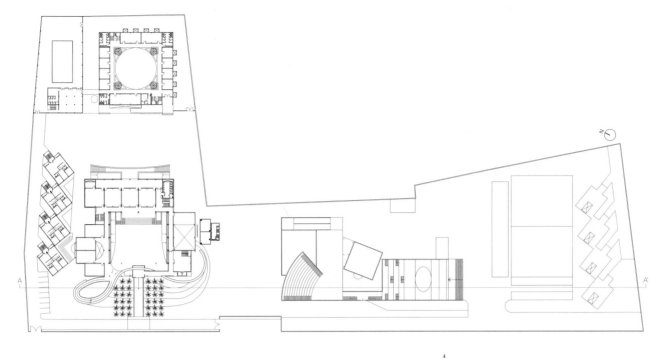

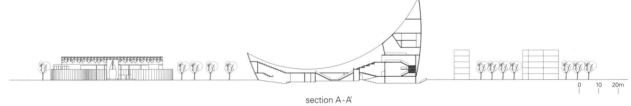

section A-A'

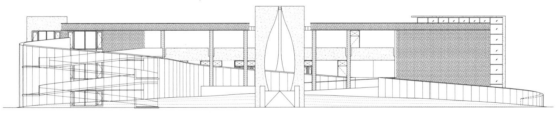

south-west elevation

south-east elevation

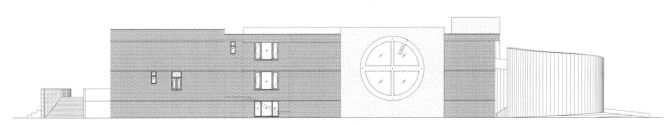

north-west elevation

이슬람 리더쉽 교육 센터

오랜 전통의 이슬람교가 오늘날에도 신도를 비롯한 대중들에게 호소력을 갖기 위해서는 미래 세대를 위한 교육이 무엇보다 중요하다. 인도 다스나 지역에 계획된 국립 이슬람 교육 센터 캠퍼스는 종교와 국가를 아우르며 전통의 가치를 오늘날과 잇고자 한다. 이곳에서 학생들은 미래를 이끌어갈 지도자들로 거듭날 것이다.

단지는 교육관, 종교시설, 부속시설들로 이루어진다. 공간은 어떠한 장식도 배제한 채 맨 얼굴을 그대로 드러낸다. 시간과 장소에 따라 변하는 빛과 그림자만으로도, 종교가 가르치는 윤리와 아름다움을 충분히 나타낼 수 있기 때문이다.

단지 입구에 자리한 거대한 홍예문은 미신과 관습에서 해방된 사고를 상징한다. 쐐기돌이 있어야 할 곳은 비워두어 빛과 공간이 자유롭게 드나들 수 있는 틈을 만들었다.

건물들은 비슷한 형태의 원리를 취한다. 안뜰은 건물 사이를 비워 빛을 들이며, 내면을 향한 종교의 장엄한 여정을 기린다. 여기서 입구의 홍예문은 건물 전면에 자유롭게 휘감는 돌담을 붙들어, 안뜰의 기하학적 질서와 전통을 잇는다. 또한 안뜰은 건물 두 개 층 높이 사이 놓여 녹지에 최대한 접근할 수 있게 하였다.

전면의 돌담은 경직된 건물의 형태를 강렬하게 휘감으며 솟아오른다. 시각적으로 역동적인 변화를 보여주는 동시에, 작은 야자수 정원을 품어 현관 공간을 외부의 시야로부터 보호한다. 또한 건물 중심의 안뜰을 마무리 지으며, 장애인 경사로와 함께 구불구불하게 여러 뜰을 감싼다.

어학실을 비롯한 각종 교실, 교무실과 다목적 시설들은 전형적인 벽돌 건물 안에 구성된다. 건물 안에서 가르침과 교습이 이루어진다면, 밖에서는 대화와 담론을 통해서 배움이 행해진다. 중심의 안뜰을 향해 이어진 넓은 베란다는 앉아서 쉬거나 모임을 가질 수 있는 공간이 된다.

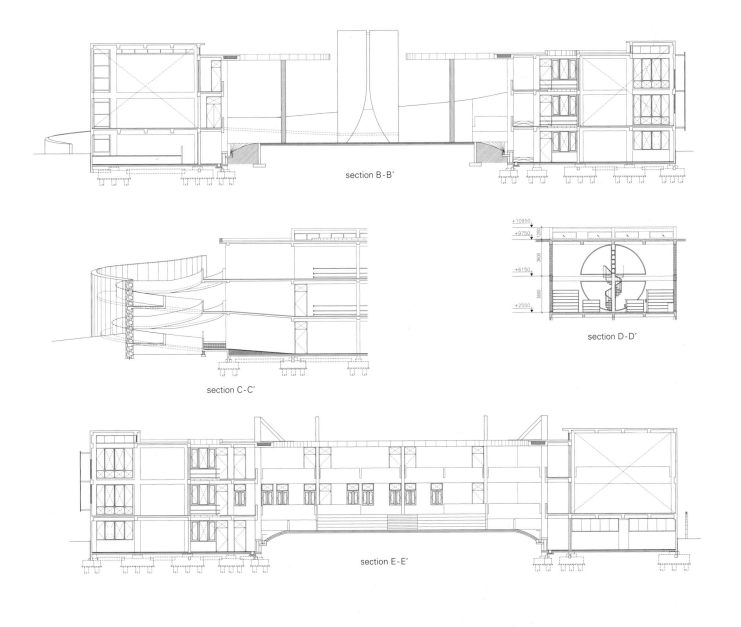

section B-B'

section C-C'

section D-D'

section E-E'

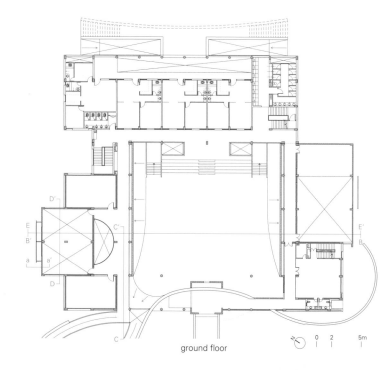

ground floor

0 2   5m

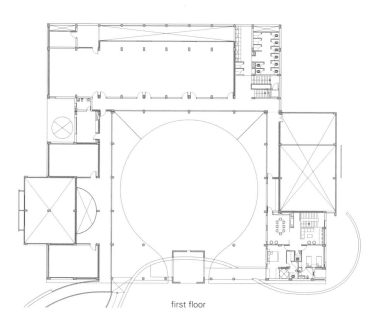

first floor

한편, 입구 현관에는 교무실, 바로 위에는 부총장을 위한 거주 공간이
마련되어 있다. 건물 내 모든 공간은 이슬람교의 교리에 따라 바깥으
로는 닫혀있으며, 오직 여러 천창을 통해서만 빛을 들인다.

이 벽돌 건물의 양쪽에서 직각으로 만나는 두 동의 건물에는 벽돌 외
벽선 바깥으로 작은 틈새 창과 커다란 원형 창을 돌출시켜 냈다. 여기
에 배치된 도서관은 전 층을 터서 내부가 3층 높이에 달한다. 석재 바
닥과 목재 구조체, 그리고 콘크리트 벽체는 재료의 특성을 그대로 살
려두었다. 커다란 원형 창을 설치해 빛을 들였다. 도서관에는 2층 높
이의 서가와 다중매체 자료 시설, 그리고 앉을 자리가 함께 마련돼, 편
안하게 사색하며 공부할 수 있다.

기도실 반대편의 다목적실은 많은 사람들이 모일 수 있는 강당이다.
이 공간에도 커다란 원형 창을 두었다. 다목적실 바로 아래층에는 식
당이 있는데, 위층에서 반전된 반원형 창들이 외부의 시선은 차단하
는 동시에 빛을 끌어 들인다. 초승달 모양의 반원형 창은 이슬람 전통
을 참조한 것이다.

건물 안에서 가르침과 교습이 이루어진다면, 밖에서는 대화와 담론
을 통해서 배움이 행해진다. 건물 전체를 덮는 콘크리트 지붕은 안뜰
을 중심으로 둥글게 돌출되어, 바깥 공간들을 가리운다. 그러나 입구
를 향해서는 열려, 고정된 관념의 틀을 깨트린다. 학생들은 이 뜰을 오
가며 대화를 나누고 어울리곤 한다. 부유하는 지붕에는 여러 세모 형
별들이 불규칙적으로 뚫려있다. 문양 윤곽을 노랗고 하얗게 칠한 것은
이슬람교와 관련한 문화에서 흔히 볼 수 있는 장식 주제이다. 빛은 이
독특한 천창을 통해 안뜰까지 들어와, 다양한 형태와 그림자를 온 종
일 드리워 혹독한 태양과 맞선다.

교정의 이 상징적인 별들은 정신을 흥미롭고 황홀하게 만드는 한편,
무엇보다 딱딱하고 엄정한 지식에 자유와 즐거움으로 균형 맞춰준다.

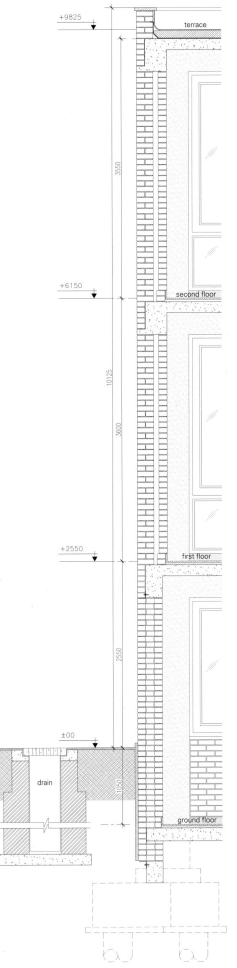

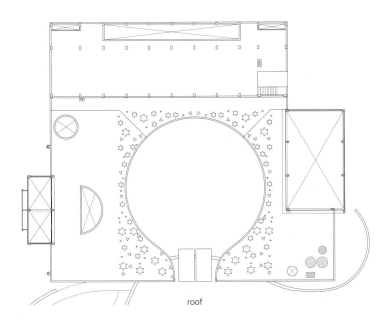

roof

Project: National Institute for Faith Leadership / Location: Dasna, India / Architects: Archohm Consults
Principal architect: Sourabh Gupta / Design team: Sanjay Rawat, Amit Sharma, Rachna Sharma, Yashveer Singh, Kriti Aggarwal
Structural engineer: Deepali Consulting engineers / Mechanical / HVAC / Engineering: NIL / Electrical engineer: Archohm Consults
Civil: Shakeel/Ved Prakash / Landscape architect: Vinyas Landscape Architect / Plumbing: Techno Engineering
Façade: Hargovind / Client: Maulana Mahmood Asad Hussain Madani / Client's firm: Sheikhul Hind Educational Charitable Trust
Site area: 24,431.9m² / Bldg. area: 4,959.4m² / Start: 2012.8 / Completion: 2014.10
Photograph: ©Andre J Fanthome (courtesy of the architect)

...chitects of 16 people, including the two AIA members, Juan Miro and Miguel Rivera. Miguel Rivera was born in San Juan, Puerto Rico. Obtained his B.Arch from the University of Puerto Rico and M.Arch from Columbia University. Was awarded the AIA National Young Architect Award in 2005. Juan Miro was born in Barcelona and studied at the Polytechnic university of Madrid. In 1989 he earned a Fulbright Scholarship to complete a post-professional Master's degree at Yale University. Is teaching at the University of Texas School of Architecture. The firm has garnered various awards, including the AR Emerging Architecture Award and Austin AIA Firm Achievement Award.

미로 리베라 아키텍츠는 16명의 직원을 둔 건축사무소로 후안 미로와 미겔 리베라가 함께 이끌고 있다. 푸에르토리코의 산 후안 출신 건축가 미겔 리베라는 푸에르토리코 대학교를 졸업한 뒤 미국으로 건너가 컬럼비아 대학교에서 건축 석사를 취득했다. 2005년에 미국 건축가 협회로부터 젊은 건축가상을 받았다. 후안 미로는 바르셀로나에서 태어나 마드리드 종합기술대학교에서 건축을 공부했으며 1989년 예일 대학교에서 석사 과정 중에 풀브라이트 장학금을 받았다. 현재 텍사스 대학교 건축학부에서 강의하고 있다. 이들은 현재 미국 건축가 협회의 정회원으로 활동하고 있으며, AIA 공로상과 AR 어워드 등 국내외에서 다양한 건축상을 받았다.

94

AREP

...s a multidisciplinary practice in transforming the city. Founded in 1997 within SNCF (the French national rail operator) by Jean-Marie Duthilleul and Etienne Tricaud - both architects and engineers - AREP Group delivers projects on different scales going from large metropolitan areas and urban districts to individual buildings and street furniture. Its reputation is based on the ability to conceive and create multimodal stations in dense urban areas, in other words mobility-related spaces housing complex uses and facing challenging technical and heritage issues. Building on this knowledge, AREP can provide effective solutions for other types of public spaces. AREP brings together 750 people and more than 30 nationalities, professionals from diverse disciplines: architects, urban planners, designers, engineers, economists, architectural programming consultants and construction operations managers. Offers their expertise in all areas of city planning and construction: multimodal hubs and railway stations, public amenities, offices, hotels and housing, shopping centres and technical facilities.

AREP은 도시 변화를 목표로 작업하는 종합건축사무소다. 건축가이자 엔지니어인 장 마리 뚜띠엘과 에티엔 트리꾸가 1997년 프랑스 국립 철도 회사인 SNCF와 함께 설립한 AREP 그룹은 넓은 대도시 지역에서부터 개별 건물, 거리 가구에 이르기까지 다양한 스케일의 도시 프로젝트를 설계한다. AREP은 조밀한 도시 지역에서 문화유산과 관련된 해법이 필요한 복합 역사 프로젝트와 공동주택단지 등을 전문으로 작업하며, 다양한 공공공간의 문제를 살피고 해결책을 효율적으로 제시한다. 전세계 750 개국 이상, 30개 이상 국적의 건축가, 도시 계획가, 디자이너, 엔지니어, 경제학자, 건축 프로그래밍 컨설턴트 및 건물 운영 관리자 등 여러 분야의 전문가들이 AREP에서 함께 일하고 있다. 기차역, 공공 시설, 사무실, 호텔, 주택, 쇼핑 센터 및 기술 시설 등 도시 계획과 건설의 모든 분야에서 전문 지식을 제공하고자 한다.

46

Tadao Ando Architect & Associates

Tadao Ando was born in Japan in 1941. Is one of the most renowned contemporary Japanese architects. Characteristics of his work contain large expanses of unadorned architectural concrete walls combined with wooden or stone floors and large windows. Active natural elements, like sun, rain, and wind are a distinctive inclusion to his style. Established Tadao Ando Architect & Associates in 1969 and was awarded the Annual Prize of Architectural Institute of Japan for "Row House in Sumiyoshi" in 1979. Has received many awards including Académie d'Architecture in 1989, The Pritzker Architecture Prize in 1995, Gold Medal of the American Institute of Architects in 2002, and Gold Medal of Union Internationale des Architectes in 2005.

다다오 안도는 1941년 일본 오사카 태생으로, 일본에서 가장 명망 높은 현대 건축가 중 하나로 꼽힌다. 르꼬르뷔지에의 건축에 흥미를 느껴 건축을 공부하게 되었으며, 1969년에 다다오 안도 아키텍트 & 어쏘시츠를 설립해 오늘날까지 현직 건축가로 활발히 활동하고 있다. 그의 건축은 해와 비, 그리고 바람과 같은 자연 요소와 독특한 방법으로 결합한다. 또한, 유리와 노출 콘크리트를 주로 사용하여 간결하고 단순하면서도 차갑지 않다. 1979년에 '스미요시 연립 주택'으로 일본 건축 학회 상을 받기 시작하여, 1989년 프랑스 건축 아카데미 대상, 1995년 프리츠커 건축상, 2002년 미국 건축가 협회 골드 메달, 2005년 국제 건축가 연합 골드 메달 등 수많은 상을 받았다.

Anna Roos

Studied architecture at the UCT(University of Cape Town) and holds a postgraduate degree from the Bartlett School of Architecture, UCL, London. Moving to Switzerland in 2000, she worked as an architect, designing buildings in Switzerland, South Africa, Australia, and Scotland. As a freelance architecture journalist since 2007, she writes for A10, Ensuite Kultur Magazin, Monocle, and Swisspearl.

아나 로스는 케이프타운 대학교를 졸업하고 런던 바틀렛 건축학교에서 석사 학위를 받았다. 2000년에 스위스로 건너가 건축가로서의 경력을 쌓기 시작해 스위스, 남아프리카, 호주, 스코틀랜드 등 여러 나라에서 다양한 건축 작업을 했다. 2007년부터는 프리랜서 건축 저널리스트로서 A10, 모노클, 스위스펄 등의 전문지에 기고해오고 있다.

158

Architecture Brio

Is an Indian design studio set up in Mumbai, 2006 by Indian architect Shefali Balwani and Dutch architect Robert Verrijt. Shefali Balwani graduated from the Center for Environmental Planning and Technology (CEPT University), India and Robert Verrijt graduated from the Technical University Delft, the Netherlands. They are focusing primarily on the fields of architecture and interior design. The House on a Stream won the award for the best residential design at the NDTV DA Awards 2013 and the JKC Architecture of the Year Award 2014. The studio was selected amongst the "AD50", the Architectural Digest India list of the most influential designers in India. In 2014, they were awarded the "Best Practice in India" at the Trends Excellence Awards 2014. The project Casa BRIO was recently awarded best residential interior at the NDTV Awards 2015.

아키텍처 브리오는 세팔리 발와니로 로버트 베리트가 2006년 인도 뭄바이에 설립한 건축사무소다. CEPT 대학교 출신의 인도 건축가 세팔리 발와니와 델프트 공대 출신의 네덜란드 건축가 로버트 베리트는 건축 및 인테리어 분야에서 활동해 왔다. '시냇물 위의 집'은 2013년 NDTV로부터 최고 주택상을 받았으며, 2014년에는 JK시멘트 사에서 주최하는 올해의 건축상을 받았다. 또한 인도에서 가장 영향력 있는 디자이너 50인에게 수여하는 AD50에 선정되기도 했다. 2014년에 Trends Excellence Awards에서 인도 최고의 건축사무소로 선정되었으며, '브리오 주택'은 2015년 NDTV에서 최고 인테리어상을 수상했다.

Gihan Karunaratne

Is a British architect and a graduate of Royal College of Arts and Bartlett School of Architecture. Has taught and lectured in architecture and urban design in UK, Sri Lanka and China. Writes and researches extensively on art, architecture and urban design. Currently is the Director of architecture for Colombo Art Biennale 2016. Has exhibited in Colombo art Biennale in 2014, Rotterdam Architecture Biennale in 2009 and the Royal Academy Summer Exhibition. Is a recipient of The Bovis and Architect Journal award for architecture and was made a Fellow of Royal Society of Arts (RSA) for Architecture, Design and Education in 2012.

기한 카루나랏뜬은 영국에서 활동하는 건축가로, 영국 왕립건축학교와 바틀렛 건축학교를 졸업했다. 영국, 스리랑카와 중국에서 건축과 도시 디자인을 가르쳐왔다. 예술, 건축과 도시 디자인에 대해 글을 쓰며 연구하고 있다. 현재 2016 콜롬보 예술 비엔날레의 건축 총감독으로 활동하고 있다. 2009 로테르담 건축 비엔날레, 2014 콜롬보 예술 비엔날레와 영국 왕립 아카데미의 여름 전시회에 참여했다. 2012년에는 영국의 아키텍츠 저널과 보비스가 주최하는 건축상을 받았으며 건축, 디자인, 교육을 위한 왕립 예술 협회의 회원이기도 하다.

78

Original Design Studio

Principal Architect, Zhang Ming ^{right} was born in Shanghai, China in 1968 and received Ph.D at the Tongji university. Is an expert of urban planning commission of Shanghai and Professor of Department of architecture, Tongji university. Design director, Zhang Zi ^{left} was born in Shanghai, China in 1969 and received M.Arch at the Tongji university. They are Class 1 Registered Architect of China.

장 밍^{오른쪽}과 장 쯔^{왼쪽}가 오리지널 디자인 스튜디오의 대표로서 함께 사무소를 이끌고 있다. 대표 건축가 장 밍은 1968년 상하이 태생으로, 통지대학교에서 박사 학위를 취득했다. 상하이 도시계획 위원회 소속으로도 활동하고 있으며, 모교에서 학생들을 가르치고 있다. 디자인 대표인 장 쯔는 1969년 상하이에서 태어나, 통지대학교에서 건축 석사 학위를 취득했다.

128

S+PS Architects

Was set up by Shilpa Gore-Shah and Pinkish Shah in 1997 for Architecture, Urban Design and Interior services. Both of them studied at the Sir J.J. College of Architecture in Mumbai and perpetuated their studies up to the Master's Degree n architecture at the University of New Mexico, Albuquerque, USA. They are registered Architects of the Council of Architecture and members of the Indian nstitute of Architects and Indian Institute of Interior Designers. Received numerous prizes from the Indian Institute of Architects Awards and NDTV Design & rchitecture Awards.

실파 고어-샤와 핀키쉬 샤는 뭄바이의 Sir J.J. 건축대학교를 졸업한 뒤 미국으로 건너가 뉴멕시코대학교에서 건축 석사 학위를 취득했다. 1997년에 건축, 도시, 인테리어 사무소인 S+PS 아키텍츠를 립했다. 두 사람은 인도 건축가 협회 공인 건축사로, 건축가 협회와 인테리어 디자이너 협회의 회원으로 활동하고 있으며 인도 건축가 협회 상과 NDTV 건축상 등을 수상했다.

170

Sameep Padora and Associates

Is a Mumbai based architecture studio led by principal architect and founder, Sameep Padora. Completed his undergraduate studies in Mumbai in 1996 followed by post-graduate studies at Cambridge, where he received a Master's Degree from the GSD Harvard in 2005. Is a member of the Academic Council at the School of Environment and Architecture(SEA), Mumbai. sP+a received the AR Emerging Architecture Award in 2011 and WAN 21 for 21 Emerging Practices in 2014. Also has been a Nominee for the BSI Swiss Architecture Award 2014. The Lattice House received Wallpaper Magazine Design Award for the Best New Private house in 2016.

인도 뭄바이에 위치한 sP+a 건축사무소를 이끌고 있는 사밉 파도라는 1996년 뭄바이에서 건축 학사 과정을 마친 뒤, 미국 케임브릿지로 건너가 하버드 건축대학원에서 2005년에 건축 석사 학위를 취득했다. 현재 뭄바이 소재의 건축환경대학교(SEA)에서 학술 위원으로 활동하고 있다. 젊은 건축가에게 수여하는 AR 어워드와 WAN 21을 수상한 바 있으며, 2014년에 BSI 스위스 건축상의 수상 후보에 오르기도 했다. 최근 작품인 래티스 주택은 월페이퍼 매거진에서 2016년 최고의 신축 주택으로 선정되었다.

144

182

Is led by two Registered Architects of USA, David Marc Schafer and Orapun Im Sarasalin Schafer with a team of architects, designers, and fabricators. David Marc Schafer graduated from the University of Arizona with B.Arch in 2000 and received MFA at the Cranbrook Academy of Art in Michigan, 2009. Orapun Im Sarasalin Schafer studied Architecture and Design Program at the University of Copenhagen and received B.Arch with Magna Cum Laude from the University of Arizona in 2003. After graduation, she received MFA at the Cranbrook Academy of Art in 2009 with David Marc Schafer. They are currently working in Bangkok and teaching at the Rangsit University in Thailand.

스튜디오메이크는 두 명의 미국 공인 건축사인 데이빗 마크 샤퍼와 오라푼 임 사라살린 샤퍼가 함께 운영하는 건축사무소다. 데이빗 샤퍼는 애리조나 대학교에서 건축을 전공하고 크랜브룩 예술학교에서 2009년에 순수미술 석사 학위를 취득했다. 오라푼 임 사라살린 샤퍼는 코펜하겐 대학교에서 건축 디자인 프로그램을 공부하고 미국으로 건너가 2003년에 애리조나 대학교 건축학부를 차석으로 졸업했다. 이후 2009년에 크랜브룩 예술학교에서 데이빗 샤퍼와 함께 순수미술 석사 학위를 받았다. 이들은 현재 태국의 방콕에 터전을 잡고 작업하며, 랑싯대학교에서 강의하고 있다.

Was established in 1995 by two principals Sanjeev Panjabi(1969) and Sangeeta Merchant(1967). Both were educated at the Academy of Architecture, Mumbai(1987~1992). Was formed when two of them got together for one project way back in 1997. Since 1987, they shared ideas, traveled together and begun to understand each other's divergent thought processes and approach to real life situations. Received the AR Awards 09 for the Commendation for EXIM Tower. Is busy with the construction and design of several residential, commercial and mixed use projects in India and Tanzania.

스파즘 디자인 아키텍츠는 인도 뭄바이 건축 아카데미 출신의 두 건축가 쌘지브 판자비와 쌘지타 머챈트가 1995년에 설립한 건축사무소다. 둘은 학창 시절부터 여러 가지 건축적인 아이디어를 공유하며 자연스레 협업해 오다가, 1997년에 한 프로젝트를 진행하면서 본격적으로 건축사무소 스파즘을 시작했다. 2009년에 AR 어워드를 수상했으며, 현재 인도와 탄자니아에서 주거 및 상업 건물 등 다양한 프로젝트의 설계 및 시공을 책임지고 있다.

Was founded in 2000 by architect Sourabh Gupta, who studied architecture at the Centre for Environmental Planning and Technology (CEPT) University at Ahmedabad, India and TU Delft, the Netherlands. From master planning of cities to designing their street signage, from farmer markets to cultural haats, hospitals to hospitality, riverfronts to residential projects, archohm has ventured into almost every typology of projects with 'design' as its main focus making it a very versatile firm. Its portfolio now spans across a diversity of sectors that include large public, social, educational, religious and cultural institutions.

인도 건축가인 수라브 굽타는 인도 아메다바드의 CEPT 대학교와 네덜란드의 델프트 공과대학교에서 건축을 공부한 뒤 2000년에 아르꼼 컨설츠를 설립했다. 도시 계획부터 도로 신호등 정비와 같은 작은 프로젝트까지, 농산물 시장과 다양한 문화 공간, 의료 시설, 수변 설계와 주택 건축 등 거의 모든 분야의 프로젝트를 담당하면서 노련한 스튜디오로 거듭났다. 현재도 대형 공공 시설과 사회, 교육, 종교, 문화 시설 등 다양한 프로젝트를 진행하고 있다.

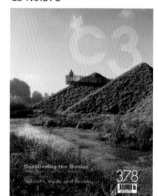

C3 No.376

C3 No.375

C3 No.374

C3 No.373

C3 No.372

C3 No.371

C3 No.370

C3 No.369

C3

No. 384

ISSN 2092-5190 / 225 x 300mm, pb / 200 pages / Color & Illustrate / English / Korean

Retreats and Escapes
Meditation

Inaugurated in 1984
Published 12 times a year

Subscription on-line at www.c3p.kr
by email to subs@c3p.kr
or please call our subscription
at +82 2 2661 2811

C3 Publishing Co.
18 GongHangDaeRo 2Gil GangSeo Seoul 07622 Korea
07622 서울시 강서구 공항대로2길 18
Tel +82 (2) 2661 2811   Fax +82 (2) 2661 2456
Editorial editor@c3p.kr   Subscription subs@c3p.kr
Advertisement ads@c3p.kr   Distribution biz@c3p.kr
www.c3p.kr

Subscription On-Line at www.c3p.kr